First World War
and Army of Occupation
War Diary
France, Belgium and Germany

36 DIVISION
Divisional Troops
76 Sanitary Section
25 June 1915 - 31 March 1917

WO95/2500/3

The Naval & Military Press Ltd
www.nmarchive.com
Published in association with The National Archives

Published by

The Naval & Military Press Ltd

Unit 10 Ridgewood Industrial Park,

Uckfield, East Sussex,

TN22 5QE England

Tel: +44 (0) 1825 749494

www.naval-military-press.com

www.nmarchive.com

This diary has been reprinted in facsimile from the original. Any imperfections are inevitably reproduced and the quality may fall short of modern type and cartographic standards.

© **Crown Copyright**
Images reproduced by permission of The National Archives, London, England, 2015.

Contents

ument type	Place/Title	Date From	Date To
ding	WO95/2500/3 76 Sanitary Section		
ding	36th Division 76th Sanitary Section Oct 1915-1917 Mar To S Army		
ding	36th Division Summarised but Not Copied 121/7432 76th Sanitary Section Vol I Oct 15		
ding	War Diary of Capt. J. Davies RAMC. O.C. 76th Sanitary Section 36th (Luster) Division. From Oct 12th 1915 to Oct 31st 1915 To The Officer i/c Adjutant General Office The Base.		
Diary	Haselles	12/10/1915	15/10/1915
Diary	Cardonette	16/10/1915	16/10/1915
Diary	Ally-Sur-Somme	16/10/1915	16/10/1915
Diary	Breilly	16/10/1915	16/10/1915
Diary	Haselles	16/10/1915	19/10/1915
Diary	Ailly Sur Somme	19/10/1915	19/10/1915
Diary	Haselles	11/10/1915	11/10/1915
Diary	Bertangles	19/10/1915	19/10/1915
Diary	Hasselles.	20/10/1915	20/10/1915
Diary	Coisy	20/10/1915	20/10/1915
Diary	Heselles	21/10/1915	21/10/1915
Diary	Vignacourt	11/10/1915	11/10/1915
Diary	Haselles	22/10/1915	22/10/1915
Diary	Domart	22/10/1915	24/10/1915
Diary	Bonneville	24/10/1915	24/10/1915
Diary	Domart	25/10/1915	25/10/1915
Diary	Domart En Ponthieu	26/10/1915	26/10/1915
Diary	St Leger	27/10/1915	27/10/1915
Diary	Berneaucourt	27/10/1915	27/10/1915
Diary	Domart	28/10/1915	28/10/1915
Diary	Flenvillers	28/10/1915	28/10/1915
Diary	Beauval	29/10/1915	29/10/1915
Diary	Domart	30/10/1915	31/10/1915
ding	36th Division Summarised but not copied 76th San Sect 36th Div Vol 2 76th Sany Section 121/7678 Nov. 15		
ding	War Diary of Capt. F. Davies O/C. 76th Sanitary Section from November 1st to November 30th 1915 Volume 2		
r Diary	Domart	01/11/1915	01/11/1915
r Diary	Permois	01/11/1915	01/11/1915
r Diary	St Ouen	01/11/1915	01/11/1915
r Diary	Domart	02/11/1915	02/11/1915
r Diary	Douellens	02/11/1915	02/11/1915
r Diary	Ribeaucourt	03/11/1915	03/11/1915
r Diary	Epecamps	03/11/1915	03/11/1915
r Diary	Domart	04/11/1915	04/11/1915
r Diary	Hem	04/11/1915	04/11/1915
r Diary	Domart	04/11/1915	04/11/1915
r Diary	Montrellet	05/11/1915	05/11/1915
r Diary	Domart	05/11/1915	06/11/1915
r Diary	Canaples	06/11/1915	06/11/1915

War Diary	Domart	07/11/1915	07/11/1915
War Diary	St Leger	07/11/1915	07/11/1915
War Diary	Domart	08/11/1915	09/11/1915
War Diary	Houdencourt	09/11/1915	09/11/1915
War Diary	Canaples	09/11/1915	09/11/1915
War Diary	Domart	09/11/1915	09/11/1915
War Diary	Rubeaucourt	09/11/1915	09/11/1915
War Diary	Rubeaucourt	09/10/1915	09/10/1915
War Diary	Beauval	10/11/1915	10/11/1915
War Diary	Gezamcourt	10/11/1915	10/11/1915
War Diary	Beauval	19/11/1915	19/11/1915
War Diary	Domart	11/11/1915	12/11/1915
War Diary	Flexacourt	12/11/1915	12/11/1915
War Diary	Domart	13/11/1915	13/11/1915
War Diary	Candas	13/11/1915	13/11/1915
War Diary	Domart	13/11/1915	13/11/1915
War Diary	Arqueves	14/11/1915	14/11/1915
War Diary	Domart	15/11/1915	18/11/1915
War Diary	Epecamps	18/11/1915	18/11/1915
War Diary	Domart	19/11/1915	19/11/1915
War Diary	Rancheval	19/11/1915	19/11/1915
War Diary	St Leger	20/11/1915	20/11/1915
War Diary	Domart	20/11/1915	20/11/1915
War Diary	St Leger	20/11/1915	20/11/1915
War Diary	Domart	21/11/1915	23/11/1915
War Diary	St Omer	23/11/1915	23/11/1915
War Diary	Domart	24/11/1915	24/11/1915
War Diary	Villers Bocage	25/10/1915	25/10/1915
War Diary	Domart	25/10/1915	25/10/1915
War Diary	Domart	26/11/1915	28/11/1915
War Diary	Pont Remy	25/11/1915	30/11/1915
Heading	Summarised but not copied No. 76 San. Sect. Dec 1915		
War Diary	Pont Remy	01/12/1915	01/12/1915
War Diary	Longue	01/12/1915	01/12/1915
War Diary	Conque-Rez	02/12/1915	02/12/1915
War Diary	Pont Remy	03/12/1915	03/12/1915
War Diary	Lomguet	03/12/1915	03/12/1915
War Diary	Bouchon	04/12/1915	04/12/1915
War Diary	Cocquerel	04/12/1915	04/12/1915
War Diary	Pont. Remy	04/12/1915	05/12/1915
War Diary	Moufliers	05/12/1915	05/12/1915
War Diary	Pont Remy	05/12/1915	06/12/1915
War Diary	Long	06/12/1915	06/12/1915
War Diary	Pont Remy	07/12/1915	07/12/1915
War Diary	Vauchelles	07/12/1915	07/12/1915
War Diary	Pont Remy	08/12/1915	09/12/1915
War Diary	Longue	10/12/1915	11/12/1915
War Diary	Vauchelles.	12/12/1915	12/12/1915
War Diary	Pont Remy	13/12/1915	17/12/1915
War Diary	Pont Remy	18/12/1916	18/12/1916
War Diary	Conquerel	19/12/1916	19/12/1916
War Diary	Borden	20/12/1915	20/12/1915
War Diary	Pont Remy	21/12/1915	22/12/1915
Heading	36th Div 76 San Sect 36th Div Vol 3 Jan/1916 Feb Dec 1916		
War Diary	Domart	05/01/1916	08/01/1916

Diary	St Hilaire		08/01/1916	08/01/1916
Diary	Canaples		09/01/1916	09/01/1916
Diary	Berneuil		10/01/1916	10/01/1916
Diary	Domart		11/01/1916	11/01/1916
Diary	Candas		12/01/1916	12/01/1916
Diary	Ribeaucourt		13/01/1916	13/01/1916
Diary	Beaumetz		14/01/1916	14/01/1916
Diary	Domart		15/01/1916	15/01/1916
Diary	Montrelet		16/01/1916	16/01/1916
Diary	Domart		17/01/1916	18/01/1916
Diary	Bernaville		18/01/1916	19/01/1916
Diary	Candas		20/01/1916	20/01/1916
Diary	Fienvillers		20/01/1916	21/01/1916
Diary	Beaumetz		22/01/1916	22/01/1916
Diary	Prouville		23/01/1916	23/01/1916
Diary	Bernaville		24/01/1916	24/01/1916
Diary	Domesmont		25/01/1916	25/01/1916
Diary	St. Ouen		26/01/1916	26/01/1916
Diary	Epe-Camps		27/01/1916	27/01/1916
Diary	Ribeaucourt		25/01/1916	25/01/1916
Diary	Berteaucourt		29/01/1916	29/01/1916
Diary	Candas		30/01/1916	30/01/1916
Diary	Vacquerie		31/01/1916	31/01/1916
Diary	Acheux		07/02/1916	09/02/1916
Diary	Lealvillers		09/02/1916	09/02/1916
Diary	Acheux		09/02/1916	16/02/1916
Diary	Lealvillers		17/02/1916	17/02/1916
Diary	Force-Ville		18/02/1916	18/02/1916
Diary	Acheux		19/02/1916	19/02/1916
Diary	Force-Ville		19/02/1916	19/02/1916
Diary	Acheux		20/02/1916	21/02/1916
Diary	Varennes		21/02/1916	21/02/1916
Diary	Acheux		21/02/1916	24/02/1916
Diary	Acheux		25/06/1915	25/06/1915
Diary	Clairfaye		25/06/1915	25/06/1915
Diary	Acheux		27/02/1916	28/02/1916
Diary	Leal Villers		28/02/1916	28/02/1916
Diary	Acheux		29/02/1916	29/02/1916
ding	War Diaries of 76th Sanitary Section-For the months of March and April 1916-36th Division			
ding	War Diary of Capt F. Davies R.A.M.C. O.C. 76th Sanitary Section 36th Division. To The Officer i/c Adjutant Generals Office Base. March 1916 76 San Sec Vol 4			
r Diary	Vauchelles		01/03/1916	01/03/1916
r Diary	Acheux		02/03/1916	02/03/1916
r Diary	Force-Ville		02/03/1916	02/03/1916
r Diary	Varennes		03/03/1916	03/03/1916
r Diary	Acheux		04/03/1916	05/03/1916
r Diary	Englebelmer		06/03/1916	06/03/1916
r Diary	Mailly Maillet		07/03/1916	07/03/1916
r Diary	Acheux		08/03/1916	08/03/1916
r Diary	Liel-Villers		08/03/1916	08/03/1916
r Diary	Bertrancourt		09/03/1916	09/03/1916
r Diary	Mailly-Maillet		09/03/1916	09/03/1916
r Diary	Acheux		10/03/1916	11/03/1916

War Diary	Mailly Maillet	12/03/1916	12/03/1916
War Diary	Arqueves.	13/03/1916	13/03/1916
War Diary	Leal-Villers	13/03/1916	13/03/1916
War Diary	Acheux	14/03/1916	14/03/1916
War Diary	Martinsart	15/03/1916	15/03/1916
War Diary	Beaussart.	16/03/1916	16/03/1916
War Diary	Forceville	17/03/1916	17/03/1916
War Diary	Acheux	17/03/1916	18/03/1916
War Diary	Martinsart	19/03/1916	29/03/1916
War Diary	Hapton Ville	30/03/1916	31/03/1916
Heading	War Diary of Capt F. Davies R.A.M.C. O.C. 76th Sanitary Section. 36th Division To The Officer i/c Adjutant Generals Office at the Base April 1916 76 San Sec Vol 5		
War Diary	Harponville	01/04/1916	05/04/1916
War Diary	Leal-Villers	05/04/1916	05/04/1916
War Diary	Harpon-Ville	06/04/1916	07/04/1916
War Diary	Martinsart	08/04/1916	08/04/1916
War Diary	Toutencourt	09/04/1916	09/04/1916
War Diary	Leal-Villers.	10/04/1916	10/04/1916
War Diary	Harpon-Ville	11/04/1916	11/04/1916
War Diary	Puchevillers	12/04/1916	12/04/1916
War Diary	Varennes.	13/04/1916	13/04/1916
War Diary	Force-Ville	14/04/1916	14/04/1916
War Diary	Harpon-Ville	15/04/1916	16/04/1916
War Diary	Hendauville	17/04/1916	21/04/1916
War Diary	Foutencourt	22/04/1916	22/04/1916
War Diary	Puchevillers	22/04/1916	22/04/1916
War Diary	Hedauville	23/04/1916	24/04/1916
War Diary	Martinsart	25/04/1916	25/04/1916
War Diary	Forceville	26/04/1916	26/04/1916
War Diary	Varennes	26/04/1916	26/04/1916
War Diary	Hedauville	27/04/1916	27/04/1916
War Diary	Puchevillers	27/04/1916	27/04/1916
War Diary	Harponville	27/04/1916	27/04/1916
War Diary	Hedauville	28/04/1916	29/04/1916
Heading	War Diary of Capt F. Davies R.A.M.C. O.C. 76th Sanitary Sec 36th Division To The Officer. i/c Adjutant Generals Office. Base. 76 San Sec Vol 6		
War Diary	Hedauville	01/05/1916	11/05/1916
War Diary	Puchvillers	12/05/1916	12/05/1916
War Diary	Harponville	13/05/1916	13/05/1916
War Diary	Forceville	14/05/1916	14/05/1916
War Diary	Varennes	15/05/1916	15/05/1916
War Diary	Hedauville	16/05/1916	16/05/1916
War Diary	Forceville	17/05/1916	17/05/1916
War Diary	Lealvillers	18/05/1916	18/05/1916
War Diary	Hedauville Wood	19/05/1916	19/05/1916
War Diary	Harponville	20/05/1916	20/05/1916
War Diary	Hedauville	21/05/1916	22/05/1916
War Diary	Varennes	23/05/1916	23/05/1916
War Diary	Forceville	24/05/1916	24/05/1916
War Diary	Harponville	25/05/1916	25/05/1916
War Diary	Varennes	26/05/1916	26/05/1916
War Diary	Lealvillers	27/05/1916	27/05/1916
War Diary	Hedauville	28/05/1916	29/05/1916

War Diary	Forceville	30/05/1916	30/05/1916
War Diary	Varennes	31/05/1916	31/05/1916
War Diary	Harponville	31/05/1916	31/05/1916
Heading	War Diary O.C. 76th Sanitary Section June 30th 1916 76 San Sec. Vol 7 June 1916		
War Diary	Hedauville	01/06/1916	01/06/1916
War Diary	Forceville	02/06/1916	02/06/1916
War Diary	Varennes	03/06/1916	03/06/1916
War Diary	Harponville	04/06/1916	04/06/1916
War Diary	Lealvillers	05/06/1916	05/06/1916
War Diary	Englebelmer	06/06/1916	06/06/1916
War Diary	Hedauville Wood.	07/06/1916	07/06/1916
War Diary	Varennes	08/06/1916	08/06/1916
War Diary	Clairfaye	09/06/1916	09/06/1916
War Diary	Lealvillers	10/06/1916	10/06/1916
War Diary	Varennes	11/06/1916	11/06/1916
War Diary	Forceville	12/06/1916	12/06/1916
War Diary	Varennes	13/06/1916	13/06/1916
War Diary	Hedauville Wood	17/06/1916	17/06/1916
War Diary	Harponville	15/06/1916	15/06/1916
War Diary	Varennes	16/06/1916	16/06/1916
War Diary	Forceville	17/06/1916	17/06/1916
War Diary	Hedauville Wood	18/06/1916	18/06/1916
War Diary	Lealvillers	19/06/1916	19/06/1916
War Diary	Hedauville	20/06/1916	20/06/1916
War Diary	Varennes	21/09/1916	21/09/1916
War Diary	Clairfaye	22/09/1916	22/09/1916
War Diary	Hedauville	23/06/1916	23/06/1916
War Diary	Harponville	24/06/1916	24/06/1916
War Diary	Forceville	25/06/1916	25/06/1916
War Diary	Lealvillers	26/06/1916	26/06/1916
War Diary	Hedauville	27/06/1916	27/06/1916
War Diary	Varennes	28/06/1916	28/06/1916
War Diary	Hedauville	29/06/1916	30/06/1916
Heading	War Diary of O.C. 76th Sanitary Section July 1916 36 July 76 San Sec Vol 8		
War Diary	Hedauville	01/07/1916	06/07/1916
War Diary	Rubempre	07/07/1916	09/07/1916
War Diary	Bernaville	10/07/1916	11/07/1916
War Diary	Bleringham	12/07/1916	12/07/1916
War Diary	Tilques	13/07/1916	14/07/1916
War Diary	Setques	15/07/1916	15/07/1916
War Diary	Watten	16/07/1916	16/07/1916
War Diary	Ganspette	17/07/1916	17/07/1916
War Diary	Moulle	18/07/1916	18/07/1916
War Diary	Houlle	18/07/1916	18/07/1916
War Diary	Salperwick	18/07/1916	18/07/1916
War Diary	Eperlecques	20/07/1916	20/07/1916
War Diary	Tournehem	20/07/1916	20/07/1916
War Diary	Esquelbeck	21/07/1916	22/07/1916
War Diary	Montnoir	23/07/1916	24/07/1916
War Diary	Bailleul	25/07/1916	25/07/1916
War Diary	Steenwerche	25/07/1916	25/07/1916
War Diary	Montnoir	26/07/1916	26/07/1916
War Diary	Bailleul	26/07/1916	26/07/1916
War Diary	Westhof Farm	26/07/1916	26/07/1916

War Diary	Kortepyp Camp	27/07/1916	27/07/1916
War Diary	Red Lodge	27/07/1916	27/07/1916
War Diary	Bailleul	28/07/1916	30/07/1916
War Diary	Kurte Pipcamp	31/07/1916	31/07/1916
War Diary	Red Lodge	31/07/1916	31/07/1916
War Diary	Westhof Farm	31/07/1916	31/07/1916
War Diary	Bailleul	31/07/1916	31/07/1916
Heading	War Diary of O.C. 76th Sanitary Section August 1916		
War Diary	Kortepyp	01/08/1916	01/08/1916
War Diary	Aldershot Huts	01/08/1916	01/08/1916
War Diary	Red Lodge	01/08/1916	01/08/1916
War Diary	Dranoutre	01/08/1916	01/08/1916
War Diary	Bailleul	01/08/1916	02/08/1916
War Diary	Neuve Eglise	02/08/1916	02/08/1916
War Diary	Romarin	02/08/1916	02/08/1916
War Diary	Bailleul	02/08/1916	03/08/1916
War Diary	Neuve Eglise	04/08/1916	04/08/1916
War Diary	Bailleul	05/08/1916	05/08/1916
War Diary	Westhof Farm	05/08/1916	05/08/1916
War Diary	Fletre	05/08/1916	05/08/1916
War Diary	Mont Noir	06/08/1916	06/08/1916
War Diary	Bailleul	07/08/1916	07/08/1916
War Diary	Dranoutre	07/08/1916	07/08/1916
War Diary	Bailleul	08/08/1916	08/08/1916
War Diary	Neuve Eglise Road	08/08/1916	08/08/1916
War Diary	Bailleul	09/08/1916	09/08/1916
War Diary	Kortepyp Camp	09/08/1916	09/08/1916
War Diary	Kortepyp	10/08/1916	10/08/1916
War Diary	Trenches	10/08/1916	10/08/1916
War Diary	Bailleul	11/08/1916	11/08/1916
War Diary	Kortepyp	12/08/1916	12/08/1916
War Diary	Bailleul	12/08/1916	12/08/1916
War Diary	Romarin	13/08/1916	13/08/1916
War Diary	Dranoutre	13/08/1916	13/08/1916
War Diary	Petit Pont	14/08/1916	14/08/1916
War Diary	Bailleul	15/08/1916	15/08/1916
War Diary	Neuve Eglise	15/08/1916	15/08/1916
War Diary	Kortepyp	15/08/1916	15/08/1916
War Diary	Red Lodge	15/08/1916	15/08/1916
War Diary	Fletre	15/08/1916	15/08/1916
War Diary	Bailleul	17/08/1916	17/08/1916
War Diary	Westhof Farm	17/08/1916	17/08/1916
War Diary	Kortepyp Camp	18/08/1916	18/08/1916
War Diary	St Jans Cappel	19/08/1916	19/08/1916
War Diary	Bailleul	19/08/1916	20/08/1916
War Diary	Petit Pont	21/08/1916	21/08/1916
War Diary	Red Lodge	21/08/1916	21/08/1916
War Diary	St Jans Cappel	22/08/1916	22/08/1916
War Diary	Bailleul	22/08/1916	22/08/1916
War Diary	St Jans Cappel	22/08/1916	23/08/1916
War Diary	Petit Port	23/08/1916	23/08/1916
War Diary	St Jans Cappel	24/08/1916	24/08/1916
War Diary	Trenches	24/08/1916	24/08/1916
War Diary	Bailleul	25/08/1916	25/08/1916
War Diary	Kortepyp Camp.	25/08/1916	25/08/1916
War Diary	St Marie Cappel	25/08/1916	25/08/1916

War Diary	Bailleul	26/08/1916	26/08/1916
War Diary	St Jans Cappel	27/08/1916	27/08/1916
War Diary	Westhof Farm	27/08/1916	27/08/1916
War Diary	Bailleul	27/08/1916	27/08/1916
War Diary	Red Lodge	28/08/1916	28/08/1916
War Diary	Bailleul	29/08/1916	29/08/1916
War Diary	St Jans Cappel	30/08/1916	30/08/1916
War Diary	Neuve Eglise	30/08/1916	30/08/1916
War Diary	Mont Noir	31/08/1916	31/08/1916
War Diary	Bailleul	31/08/1916	31/08/1916
War Diary	St Jans Cappel	31/08/1916	31/08/1916
Heading	War Diary Of. Capt. J. Davies. RAMC. O.C. 76th Sanitary Section 30th September 1916 36th Div. Sept 1916		
War Diary	Bailleul	01/09/1916	01/09/1916
War Diary	St Jans Cappel	01/09/1916	01/09/1916
War Diary	Petit Pont	02/09/1916	02/09/1916
War Diary	St Jans Cappel	03/09/1916	03/09/1916
War Diary	Bailleul	04/09/1916	04/09/1916
War Diary	Trois Rois	05/09/1916	05/09/1916
War Diary	Westhof Farm	06/09/1916	06/09/1916
War Diary	Neuve Eglise	07/09/1916	07/09/1916
War Diary	Dranoutre	08/09/1916	08/09/1916
War Diary	St Marie Cappel	09/09/1916	09/09/1916
War Diary	Dranoutre	10/09/1916	11/09/1916
War Diary	Wakefield Huts	12/09/1916	12/09/1916
War Diary	Neuve Eglise	13/09/1916	13/09/1916
War Diary	St Jans Cappel	14/09/1916	14/09/1916
War Diary	Bailleul	15/09/1916	15/09/1916
War Diary	Dranoutre	16/09/1916	16/09/1916
War Diary	St Jans Cappel	17/09/1916	17/09/1916
War Diary	Locre	18/09/1916	18/09/1916
War Diary	Mont Noir	19/09/1916	19/09/1916
War Diary	Kemmel	20/09/1916	20/09/1916
War Diary	Dranoutre	21/09/1916	21/09/1916
War Diary	Kortypip Camp.	22/09/1916	22/09/1916
War Diary	St Marie Cappel	23/09/1916	23/09/1916
War Diary	Dranoutre	24/09/1916	25/09/1916
War Diary	Bailleul	26/09/1916	26/09/1916
War Diary	Kandahar Farm	27/09/1916	27/09/1916
War Diary	Dranoutre	28/09/1916	28/09/1916
War Diary	Mont Noir	29/09/1916	29/09/1916
War Diary	Stinking Farm	30/09/1916	30/09/1916
Heading	War Diary Of Capt J. Davies. R.A.M.C. O.C. 76th Sanitary Section 31st October 1916 Vol 11		
War Diary	Bailleul	01/10/1916	31/10/1916
Heading	36th Div War Diary of Capt. J. Davies. R.A.M.C. O.C. 76th Sanitary Section November 1916 Vol 12		
War Diary	Bailleul	01/11/1916	30/11/1916
Heading	36th Div War Diary of Capt E. Sprawson R.A.M.C. O.C. 76th Sanitary Section 31st December 1916 Vol 13		
War Diary	Bailleul	01/12/1916	31/12/1916
Heading	36th Div War Diary Of Capt E. Sprawson R.A.M.C. O.C. 76th Sanitary Section 31st January 1917 Vol 14		
War Diary	Bailleul	01/01/1917	31/01/1917

Heading	36th Div War Diary of Capt E. Sprawson. R.A.M.C. O.C. 76th Sanitary Section February 1917 Vol 17		
War Diary	Bailleul	01/02/1917	28/02/1917
Heading	War Diary of Capt E.C. Sprawson. R.A.M.C.T O.C. 76th Sanitary Section 31st March 1917 Vol 16		
War Diary	Bailleul	01/03/1917	31/03/1917

Wolaś/2500/3

76 Sanitary Section

36TH DIVISION

76TH SANITARY SECTION
OCT 1915 - ~~DEC 1916~~
1917 MAR

To 5 ARMY

121/7433

36th Division

Summarised but not copied

76th Sanitary Section
vol I
Oct 15

Inner Cover

CONFIDENTIAL

War Diary of
Capt. J. Davis. R.A.M.C.
O.C 76th Sanitary Section
36th (Ulster) Division.

From Oct 12th 1915 to Oct 31st 1915

To
The Officer
I/c Adjutant Generals Office.
The Base.

Army Form C. 2118

WAR DIARY
or
INTELLIGENCE SUMMARY
(Erase heading not required.)

Instructions regarding War Diaries and Intelligence Summaries are contained in F. S. Regs., Part II. and the Staff Manual respectively. Title Pages will be prepared in manuscript.

Place	Date	Hour	Summary of Events and Information	Remarks and references to Appendices
Naville	12/10/15	10 a.m.	Ordered by A.D.M.S. 36th Division to go to BERTANGLES and disinfect a ward of the 109th Field Ambulance in which a case of Scarlet Fever had occurred. Took my motor lorry with a Sergeant and three men and disinfected the ward with formalin, afterwards disinfected all the billets of the men of the 109th Field Ambulance.	
Naville	14/10/15	11 a.m.	A case of Scarlet Fever having occurred in the 9th Royal Inniskilling Fusiliers at BERTANGLES. I went over to see the M.O. in charge of the regiment, made arrangements with him to isolate his contacts and disinfected the billets with formalin in which the men had been.	
	14/10/15	2 p.m.	A case of German measles having occurred in the 1/1 London Brigade R.F.A. Ammunition Column at ST SAUVEUR, I went over and saw the M.O. in charge about isolating his contacts and disinfected the billets in which the man had been.	

WAR DIARY
or
INTELLIGENCE SUMMARY
(Erase heading not required.)

Army Form C. 2118

Place	Date	Hour	Summary of Events and Information	Remarks and references to Appendices
Heuelles	14/10/15	5 p.m.	Ordered to go and disinfect a ward of the 109th Field Ambulance at BERTANGLES in which a number of cases of Scabies had been. This was done with Formalin.	
"	15/10/15	10 a.m.	Three bundles of blankets were sent me for disinfection from the 110th Field Ambulance. Of men who had suffered from Scabies. I disinfected these in the portable hot disinfector, and returned them to the 110th Field Ambulance. The Ambulance stated [?] that the blankets in use were disinfected with Formalin.	
"	"	2 pm	Ordered to go to VIGNACOURT to inspect the Sanitary arrangements of the 110th Field Ambulance. Advised that the pail system should be used instead of the trench for the Latrines, and that the Urine pit should be dug six feet deep and filled with rubble & that perforated biscuit tins be placed at the top of the pit with tunnels leading to them made of tin or zinc for the men to urinate in. Advised that an unused greenhouse in the grounds of the Hospital be made	

WAR DIARY
or
INTELLIGENCE SUMMARY

(Erase heading not required.)

Army Form C. 2118

Place	Date	Hour	Summary of Events and Information	Remarks and references to Appendices
Naours	15/10/15	2 p.m.	into a drying room for the men's clothes when washed. The Sanitary arrangements of the Field Ambulance were on the whole good.	
"		4 p.m.	Seven men kits arrived for disinfection from the 109th Field Ambulance, all cases of scabies. They were disinfected in the hot disinfector & returned. It's Ambulance was disinfected with Formalin that brought the kits.	
CARDON-NETTE	16/10/15	11.15 a.m.	A case of German measles having occurred in the 11th Royal Inniskilling Fusiliers I went over to CARDONNETTE and saw the M.O in charge of the regiment about the isolation of his contacts and disinfected the billets in which the man had been with Formalin. I also inspected the sanitary arrangements of this Regiment and found them most excellent.	
AILLY-SUR-SOMME		2 p.m.	Went to Ailly-sur-Somme and inspected the billets and sanitary arrangements of the Mobile Veterinary Section and found them in good order.	

WAR DIARY
or
INTELLIGENCE SUMMARY

(Erase heading not required.)

Army Form C. 2118

Place	Date	Hour	Summary of Events and Information	Remarks and references to Appendices
Breilly	16/10/15	3/15 pm	Went to BREILLY and inspected the billets and sanitary arrangements of the 10th Div Ammunition Column. Found the men were short of straw for sleeping on, reported this to the O.C. and to the A.D.M.S. 36th Division on my return. The sanitary arrangements of the Ammunition Column were good.	
Flxxelles	16/10/15	5 pm	Inspected Camp and Sanitary arrangements of Army Ordinance Corps near Flxxelles Station and found all correct.	
"		2 pm	Disinfected blankets and clothes of men suffering from scabies in the boot disinfector. Sent by the 108th and 109th Field Ambulances. 92 Ambulances were disinfected with formalin before returning.	
Flxxelles	17/10/15	9 a-m	Some cases of diarrhoea having occurred among the men stationed at Head Quarters. I visited the cook house of the Headquarters Staff with the A.D.M.S. of the 36th Division. The cause was probably due to excessive eating of unripe apples and pears. Inspected the	

WAR DIARY or INTELLIGENCE SUMMARY

Army Form C. 2118

Place	Date	Hour	Summary of Events and Information	Remarks and references to Appendices
Flaselles	17/10/15	9 a.m.	Sanitary arrangements at Head Quarters and found all in good order	
"	"	11 a.m.	Inspected the Sanitary Arrangements and latrines of the A.S.C. Coy in FLASELLES and ordered latrines to be dug further away from the billets and empty biscuit tins to be placed for men to urinate in at night, outside the billets. The tins to be emptied in the running into the urine pit near the latrines.	
"	"	2 p.m.	Saw the ADMS Mobile Division and suggested that the pail system for latrines be used in the whole division, as the trench system causes much fouling of the grounds, and in many of the billets there is not much ground for digging trench latrines.	
"	"	3 p.m.	Disinfected three bundles of clothes of men suffering from Scabies in the box disinfector, sent in by the 189th Field Ambulance. 9 Do Ambulance was also disinfected before returning.	

WAR DIARY
or
INTELLIGENCE SUMMARY

Army Form C. 2118

Place	Date	Hour	Summary of Events and Information	Remarks and references to Appendices
Flixecourt	18/10/15	9 a.m.	Proceeded to VIGNACOURT to arrange with OC 110th Field Ambulance as to what sanitary arrangements he proposes to adopt when opening his Divisional Rest Station which he has been ordered to do. Arranged sites for latrines for Officers and men, cook house, bath house, ablution room, urine pits and incinerator. The pail system of latrines is to be adopted and all fæcal matter to be burnt in the incinerator. Left a sergeant and three men to disinfect the Mairie to OC 110th Field Ambulance for taken over as a hospital.	
"	"	2 p.m.	Some hundreds of clothes of men suffering from scabies were sent in from the 109th Field Ambulance. These were disinfected in its hot disinfector and the ambulance disinfected before returning with formalin spray.	
Flixecourt	19/10/15	2 p.m.	Proceeded to AILLY SUR SOMME to inspect billets and sanitary arrangements of 1st Supply Column A.S.C. The men were using public urinals, which is contrary to Divisional orders. I told the O.C.	

Army Form C. 2118

WAR DIARY
or
INTELLIGENCE SUMMARY
(Erase heading not required.)

Instructions regarding War Diaries and Intelligence Summaries are contained in F. S. Regs., Part II. and the Staff Manual respectively. Title Pages will be prepared in manuscript.

(1) ZJ.

Place	Date	Hour	Summary of Events and Information	Remarks and references to Appendices
Ailly Sur Somme	10/10/15	3 p.m.	Men must be stopped and kept & proper wire for it must be clean. The billets were clean and in good order.	
Flesselles	11	4.30 p.m.	Saw number of cases of men suffering from Scabies were sent in from the 109th Field Ambulance, their clothes disinfected in the hot disinfecter and the Ambulance disinfected by formalin spray before returning.	
"	11	4/45 p.m.	Inspected the billets of the Mechanical Transport stationed here. The billets were clean and in good order, the Sanitary arrangements were also good.	
BERTAN- GLES	"	3 p.m.	A telegram was received from the O.C. 109th Field Ambulance asking that a hut at BERTANGLES lately occupied by scabies patients might be disinfected. A sergeant and three men were sent out and the hut was also infected by formalin spray.	

1875 Wt. W593/826 1,000,000 4/15 J.B.C. & A. A.D.S.S./Forms/C. 2118.

WAR DIARY
or
INTELLIGENCE SUMMARY

(Erase heading not required.)

Army Form C. 2118

Place	Date	Hour	Summary of Events and Information	Remarks and references to Appendices
Haroelles	20/10/15	11 a.m.	Ordered to go with the D.A.D.M.S. 36th Division to SEPTENVILLE to inspect the billets and the sanitary arrangements of the 108th Field Ambulance. The Billets were clean and in good order. The sanitary arrangements were excellent. The latrines are at present on the French system, it would be better if the pail system was used as soon as pails can be got.	
"		2 p.m.	A bundle of blankets and clothes of mess soffering from scabies was sent in by the 108th Field Ambulance. The blankets & clothes were disinfected before the Disinfector and the Ambulance disinfected before returning	
COISY	"	4 p.m.	Proceeded with the D.A.D.M.S. 36th Division to COISY to inspect the billets and sanitary arrangements of the 109th Field Ambulance, who had gone there yesterday 19/10/15. The billets were found to be clean and in a good state. Arrangements were made to have a place in one of the farm sheds made into a bath house for the men. Three boilers having been purchased for the purpose. An incinerator is to be	

Army Form C. 2118

WAR DIARY
or
INTELLIGENCE SUMMARY
(Erase heading not required.)

Place	Date	Hour	Summary of Events and Information	Remarks and references to Appendices
COISY	20/10/15	5 p.m.	erected to turn all forced ratlle as well as cat rubbish. Up pail system of latrines to be established, and an athletic room for men to be made in a shed adjoining their billets.	
Flixelles	21/10/15	10 a.m.	Received from O.C. 109th Field Ambulance 20 Blankets, 18 Shirtsleeves, 22 suits of Pyjamas to be disinfected. These had been used by patients suffering from Scabies. The Blankets and Pyjamas were disinfected in the Bot Disinfector & the Shirtsleeves sprayed with Jeomein. The Ambulance was disinfected before being sent back.	
VIGNA-COURT	11	3 p.m.	Ordered by A.D.M.S. 36th Division to proceed to NONACOURT to enquire into the suppression of 11 kits of men sent down for disinfection. I proceeded there and found that the kits had been sent to the 110th Field Ambulance from the 109th Field Ambulance, to whom the kits belonged. They had been disinfected by an on 19/10/15 at 4-30 p.m. The men had been transferred from the 109th Field Ambulance to the 110th Field Ambulance without their kits.	

Army Form C. 2118

WAR DIARY
or
INTELLIGENCE SUMMARY
(Erase heading not required.)

Place	Date	Hour	Summary of Events and Information	Remarks and references to Appendices
Moelles	22/10/15	9.6 a.m.	Having had orders to proceed with my Unit to DOMART. I ordered all latrines to be cleaned, all latrine pits be filled in, also pisse-pits and refuse pits. This was done and all billets were clean before 11 a.m. when we left.	
"	"	11 a.m.	Proceeded to DOMART with my Unit at which place we arrived at 3 p.m.	
Domart	"	3 p.m.	Took over Billets for my men and got a shed for my tools and disinfecting apparatus, a stall for my horse and a place for my motor lorry. Saw my men had their food and reported to the A.D.M.S.	
Domart	23/10/15	9 a.m.	Interviewed with Censor, Hornalls and plans of the Office of the A.D.M.S. 36th Division which was in a very dirty and insanitary condition.	
"	"	11 a.m.	Visited the Billets of the Head Quarters Staff in the market place and found the kitchen in a very dirty + insanitary condition. The yards also were very insanitary, ordered an incinerator to be built, a refuse pit to be made, a urine pit to be made, latrines and an urine pit to be dug.	
"	"	2:30 p.m.	Visited the Billets of the 36th Div. Signal Company and advised on the sanitary measures required, latrines to be dug, urine deepers, urinals	

Army Form C. 2118

WAR DIARY
or
INTELLIGENCE SUMMARY
(Erase heading not required.)

Place	Date	Hour	Summary of Events and Information	Remarks and references to Appendices
DORANT	23/10/15	2-30 p.m.	To be made. Kitchens & the pits in a different place & proper pit dug.	
"	24/10/15	10 a.m.	Visited BHQ billets of the 36th Div. by that Bve. and arrived on its sanitary condition. Too many latrines had been dug. The kitchens to be cleaned up and a drain which had overflowed owing to a stoppage, to be cleaned out. Proper grease pits to be dug. The billets themselves to be thoroughly cleaned up as the troops who had last occupied them had left them in a very dirty and insanitary condition.	
BONNE-VILLE	"	3-30 p.m.	A letter having been received from the A.D.M.S. 13th/14th London Brigade R.F.A. by the A.D.M.S. 36th Division, stating that the billets appointed to his Brigade had been left in a very insanitary condition by the troops lately occupying them. I was ordered to go to BONNEVILLE and report on their state. I went over and found the billets in a very bad state, latrine trenches had not been filled in, & were the urine pits. Manure was not was found inturned in various corners of the yards and in the billets. The whole village & the places in the village which had been used as billets were in a poor state.	

Army Form C. 2118

WAR DIARY
or
INTELLIGENCE SUMMARY
(Erase heading not required.)

Instructions regarding War Diaries and Intelligence Summaries are contained in F.S. Regs., Part II. and the Staff Manual respectively. Title Pages will be prepared in manuscript.

Place	Date	Hour	Summary of Events and Information	Remarks and references to Appendices
BONNEVILLE	24/10/15	4/30 p.m.	Was in Car thirty-three and insanitary condition. Uncovered food. Went head the call over the billets and toy inks, waste paper and empty tins also. I showed the M.O. % on the sanitation of his billets and advised, making a report to the A.D.M.S. 36th Division.	
Domart	25/10/15	9.30 a.m.	Visited the Billets of the Head Quarter Staff and again found him in an insanitary condition. Reported the Battle to the A.D.M.S. 36th Division and to the Camp Commandant.	
"	"	11 a.m.	Visited the Billets of the 36th Div. Signal Coy. R.E. and found the billets in a dirty condition. Reported to the A.D.M.S. 36th Division and to the O.C.	
"	"	12/30 p.m.	Visited the Billets of the 36th Div. Cyclist Coy. and found the billets, kitchens and yards very dirty and insanitary. Reported to the A.D.M.S. 36th Division and to the O.C. Weather fine cold in morning & evenings	

WAR DIARY or INTELLIGENCE SUMMARY

Army Form C. 2118

Place	Date	Hour	Summary of Events and Information	Remarks and references to Appendices
DOMART EN PONTHIEU	26/10/15	10 a.m.	Ordered by the A.D.M.S. 36th Division to proceed to BERNEAUCOURT and report on the Billets and Sanitation of the 10th Royal Irish Rifles. I found the Billets in fair condition, but the yards were very dirty. Ordered the 14th cleared up, most of the Church huts to be burnt and then buried. The latrines in billets were too small in size and not deep enough, ordered these to be made six feet long, two feet broad and six feet deep. Urinals were not made, these to be built. Refuse pits not sufficient, these made four feet square and four feet deep. Straw in billets to be well shaken up when men leave billets in morning and the pitched against the walls of the billets, the centre of the floor of billets to be brushed out every morning. No bread, meat etc to be kept in same billets but to be stored in their action bags. Weather wet + cold.	

WAR DIARY
or
INTELLIGENCE SUMMARY

Army Form C. 2118

Place	Date	Hour	Summary of Events and Information	Remarks and references to Appendices
ST LEGER	27/10/15	10 a.m.	Inspected the billets of the 9th Royal Irish Rifles at ST LEGER, most of the billets were good, but one in the main street I advised should be vacated as it was insanitary. The sanitation of the billets was on the whole good but incinerators & refuse pits wanted shaking in a number of billets.	
BERNEAU-COURT	"	12/30 p.m.	Inspected the new buildings that the 110th Field Ambulance have taken over for a Hospital. The buildings are good & in good repair. I disinfected a number of the rooms with Creosol & lent them wood wool with Kerosene. A big incinerator is being built for burning everything, & a new dry earth system of latrines is to be used in the Ambulance. The weather wet & cold.	
DOMART	28/10/15	10 a.m.	Disinfected with Creosol a Café in the Market Place which has been taken over as a Reception Room. Iron rooms in the Café. Lamps have been taken to make Bath Room for the men in the Café de la Halle.	
FIENVILLERS	"	12/30 p.m.	Inspected the Billets of the 11th Royal Irish Rifles. More incinerators wanted building, and latrines and urine pits are not deep enough. Arranged with the M.O./c. to have these matters remedied.	

WAR DIARY
or
INTELLIGENCE SUMMARY

(Erase heading not required.)

Army Form C. 2118

Place	Date	Hour	Summary of Events and Information	Remarks and references to Appendices
BEAU-VAL	29/10/15	11 a.m.	Inspected the 109th Field Ambulance, the billets of two sections of the Ambulance were good, but the third billet was very insanitary. A section was insanitary. I therefore condemned it & arranged with the O.C. to get another billet for this section. Also we have a very excellent billet being provided in which is to be used as quarters for the men, just up.	
DOMART	3/10/15	10 a.m.	Inspected the Guard Room, Prisoners rooms & sanitation of the Military Police. I do not consider these places sanitary and to where latrines should to-day. Have arranged with the A.P.M. to have these done immediately and to see the Liaison Officer with regard to a new Billet.	
		11 a.m.	A new Billet for the Military Police has been provided.	
		11.30 a.m.	Sentenced two of my men to ten days first field punishment for drunkenness. No 4118 Pte Rutherford R and No 53029 Pte Burns G. arranged with the A.D.M.S. 36th Division to have them men returned to the 109th Field Ambulance on completion of their sentence and the men sent me.	

WAR DIARY
or
INTELLIGENCE SUMMARY

(Erase heading not required.)

Army Form C. 2118

Place	Date	Hour	Summary of Events and Information	Remarks and references to Appendices
DOMART	30/10/15	2.30 p.m.	Visited the Billets of the Cable section R.E. The yard and surroundings of the Billet was very dirty. Arranged with the O.C. to have the yard cleaned up at once.	
DOMART	31/10/15	10 a.m.	Visited the Cable section Billets. Found the yard now clean and the Billets in good order.	
"	"	11 a.m.	Visited a civilian at a farm & café some little distance from the town, who was stated to have hidden arms by, found that he had only turned it and that there was no foundation.	
"	"	3 p.m.	Visited the Head Quarters of the Royal Artillery Divisions. The Billets &c were very dirty and proper latrines and urine pits had not been dug. I arranged with the Brigade Major to give the conviction at once.	
			Weather very cold and wet.	

36th Division
76th Sany Section

summoned but not at dijk Kans: deel.
36 li 85.
vol 2

121/7678

Nov 19f
Nov. 15

War Diary
of the 16th Sanitary Section
of Capt. J. Davis
from November 1st to November 30th
1915

Volume. 2.

WAR DIARY or INTELLIGENCE SUMMARY

Army Form C. 2118

Place	Date	Hour	Summary of Events and Information	Remarks and references to Appendices
DOMART	1/11/15	9-30 a.m	Ordered by G.O.C. 36th Division to erect models of French Latrines, Urine Pits, Soak Pits, Incinerators and Grease Traps at the Head Quarters of each Brigade. Proceeded to erect same at Divisional Head Quarters.	
PERNOIS	"	10.30 a.m	Saw the Billets and Sanitary Arrangements of the 15th Royal Irish Rifles at PERNOIS. The Billets were good but the latrines were not up to proper size being too long and not deep enough. The same applied to the urine pits. There was a want of incinerators and grease pits. The Company Officers had all erected Company baths, a most excellent idea. I arranged with the M.O'c and the Company Officer to have the sanitation of the Billets carried out in a proper manner.	
ST OUEN	"	2pm	Visited the Billets of the 94th French Mortar Battery at ST OUEN. They were in a very dirty condition and not insanitary. They were overcrowded 15 men living in a room where only 8 men should live. The floors were filthy so was the cook house. As per trip was provided the yard was full of old tins, stale bread & pieces of meat	

Army Form C. 2118

WAR DIARY
or
INTELLIGENCE SUMMARY
(Erase heading not required.)

Instructions regarding War Diaries and Intelligence Summaries are contained in F.S. Regs, Part II. and the Staff Manual respectively. Title Pages will be prepared in manuscript.

Place	Date	Hour	Summary of Events and Information	Remarks and references to Appendices
St Ouen	1/11/15	2 p.m.	In the yard were old latrines not filled in, & the cans partly dug out deep enough, as earth was thrown over excreta and as mine it had been dug. On my return to DOMART inspected the matter to the ADMS and AA & QMG, 36th Division and advised that the billets should be reacted as insanitary.	
DOMART	2/11/15	9 a.m.	Visited the new Billets occupied by Military Police and prisoners and found everything considered sanitary.	
DOUELLENS	"	10-30 a.m.	Inspected the Billets of the Supply Column at DOUELLENS and found the billets very clean and the sanitary arrangements very good.	
"	"	11-30 a.m.	Visited the Billets of the Mobile Veterinary Section at DOUELLENS the billets were clean, but the cook house needed moving badly, as it was too near a manure heap in the yard, and the latrines were not thing deep enough, a proper urine & fæces were for was not made and no	

Army Form C. 2118

WAR DIARY
or
INTELLIGENCE SUMMARY
(Erase heading not required.)

Instructions regarding War Diaries and Intelligence Summaries are contained in F. S. Regs., Part II. and the Staff Manual respectively. Title Pages will be prepared in manuscript.

Place	Date	Hour	Summary of Events and Information	Remarks and references to Appendices
DOUELLENS	2/11/15	11.30 a.m.	Incinerator trouble. Journeyed under the O.C. to have them Sanitary practices attended to immediately.	
RIBEAU-COURT	3/11/15	10 a.m.	Visited the Headquarters of the 108th Brigade and No 3 Section Signal Coy. The billets were found fairly clean, but the Sanitation was very bad. The latrines were too shallow, there were no urine pits, no incinerator, no refuse pits & no place near the cookhouse. The cook house itself was very dirty and the yard also. Reported to R.T.O. & Captain & O.C. Signal Coy. Also reported the state of affairs to the A.D.M.S. 36 Division on my return.	
LE PRE CAMPS	11	12-30 p.m.	Inspected the Billets & Sanitation of 1 to 95th Heavy Motor Battery at E PRE CAMPS and found the billets clean and the Sanitation good.	
DOMART	4/11/15	10 a.m.	92 a 61 2 mg inspected the models of trench latrines, urine pits, grease & wash pits & incinerator. Read hath-card expressed himself satisfied with every thing. I am every inspecting a Brigade of Artillery's Sanitation.	

WAR DIARY
or
INTELLIGENCE SUMMARY
(Erase heading not required.)

Army Form C. 2118

Place	Date	Hour	Summary of Events and Information	Remarks and references to Appendices
HEM	4/11/15	10 a.m.	Visited the latrines & saw the administration of the 1/3 London Brigade R. Fus. at H.E.M. The latrines were found out fairly clean, but after extrication, some pits, urinepits & incinerators wanted seeing to. Arranged with the O.C. & medical officer to have those matters carried out immediately.	
DOMART	11	3 p.m.	Many latrines were inspected also any sanitary arrangements and the models of sanitary matters viz latrines, incinerators, urinepits, grease pit & soakpit, by the Divisional Commander, Major General Huyer, who expressed himself as pleased with all he saw. The Divisional Commander ordered me to send some of my NCO's and men to the different Brigades to instruct the sanitary squads of the various battalions how to carry out the various sanitary orders. These men are to be sent on Monday, 8th November 1915.	

Army Form C. 2118

WAR DIARY
or
INTELLIGENCE SUMMARY
(Erase heading not required.)

Place	Date	Hour	Summary of Events and Information	Remarks and references to Appendices
MONTR- -ELLET	5/11/15	11 a.m.	Visited the Billets and saw the Sanitary arrangements of the 36th Divisional Train at MONTRELLET. The billets were fairly clean but the Sanitary arrangements were not at all good. I saw the M.O/c and a number of the Officers and arranged that the Billets and yards were to be immediately put into a Sanitary condition.	
DOMART	"	3 p.m.	Visited the Billets of the 36th Signal Coy, found the billets clean and the sanitary arrangements good with the exception of the incinerator which was too small. Arranged with the CO to have another incinerator built.	
DOMART	6/11/15	9-30 a.m.	Visited the Billets & saw the Sanitary arrangements of the XX Cable Coy R.E., with the ADMS 36th Division. The billets were clean and the sanitary arrangements good.	

WAR DIARY
or
INTELLIGENCE SUMMARY

(Erase heading not required.)

Army Form C. 2118

Instructions regarding War Diaries and Intelligence Summaries are contained in F.S. Regs, Part II. and the Staff Manual respectively. Title Pages will be prepared in manuscript.

Place	Date	Hour	Summary of Events and Information	Remarks and references to Appendices
DOMART	6/11/15	10 a.m.	Visited the Billets of the men employed at the Aerodrome with the A.D.M.S. 36th Division. They were found clean and the sanitary arrangements good.	
CANAPLES	11	11-30 a.m.	Visited the Billets & saw the Sanitary arrangements of the H.Q. London Brigade R.F.A. with the M.O.F. The billets were very dirty & no sanitation except in the Cook Houses. There was no attempt at sanitation except in the No. 3 Battery. Latrines were too small & in a filthy condition. No urine pits, led ten days, no refuse pits, soak pits or grease pits near the Cook houses. Reported the state of affairs to the A.D.M.S. 2 Army who wrote to Head Quarters in the Subject.	
11	11	12-30 p.m.	Inspected the Billets & sanitary arrangements of the Divisional Ammunition Column at CANAPLES. The billets were clean, the sanitary arrangements very slow poor.	

WAR DIARY
or
INTELLIGENCE SUMMARY
(Erase heading not required.)

Army Form C. 2118

Place	Date	Hour	Summary of Events and Information	Remarks and references to Appendices
DOMART	7/11/15	9.30 a.m.	Visited the Billets of the Field Ambulance Work Shops, as there was some complaint of the men having him in them and recommended to the O.C. that the staff in the billets he kept apart & have supplied, in if possible, that pure billets should be got for the men of his unit.	
S.Leger	"	2.30 p.m.	Visited the new billets of the 10th Field Ambulance at ST LEGER with the ADMS 36th Division. This ambulance has just come in from the 4th Division, relieving the 110th Field Ambulance which has gone to the 4th Division. The billets were in good order and clean. A horse in ST LEGER was taken over has a Hospital for sick officers.	
DOMART	8/11/15	10 a.m.	Visited the billets of the men in the Army Post Office and found them clean, but the were occupied by the Motor Cyclist Section were very dirty and the yard very untidy; a good deal of stock had this being used. Arranged with the O.C. to have this remedied, stated effects remedied immediately.	

WAR DIARY
or
INTELLIGENCE SUMMARY

(Erase heading not required.)

Army Form C. 2118

Place	Date	Hour	Summary of Events and Information	Remarks and references to Appendices
DOMART	8/11/15	12.30 p.m.	was called in to see a horse of 1st Dorset Killer Regiment. Pte Webber, batman to the R.M. Capt Appleton, who had shot himself in the upper leg with Capt Appleton's revolver. Found a gun shot wound of upper leg, wound of entrance on inner side of thigh, exit below knee, wound of exit on outside of upper leg, two inches above the crotch. I dressed his wounds and sent him wounded to Hospital.	
"	"	3.0 p.m.	Major J Boylan Smith D.A.D.M.S. 36th Division inspected my Billets and Sanitary arrangements, also saw over I had built for my unit.	
"	"	4.0 p.m.	Visited the Billets of the 36th Cyclist Coy. Found the Billets and Sanitary arrangements good.	

WAR DIARY
or
INTELLIGENCE SUMMARY
(Erase heading not required.)

Army Form C. 2118

Place	Date	Hour	Summary of Events and Information	Remarks and references to Appendices
DOMART	9/11/15	10 a.m.	Saw the A.A. & Q.M.G. 36th Division, who ordered me to send tomorrow November 10th, 2 N.C.O's & three men of my Unit to each Brigade in the Division to advise Battalions on sanitary matters. I detailed 3 N.C.O's and 12 men of my Unit for this purpose.	
HOUDEN- COURT	9/11/15	11 a.m.	Gave evidence (medical) at a Court of Inquiry on Pte Nicholls of 2 Inniskillin Dragoons who shot himself yesterday with a revolver at the A.P.M.'s Quarters at DOMART. Afterwards saw the Sanitary arrangements of the 10.5th Field Ambulance which were satisfactory.	
CANAPLES	"	2 p.m.	Sent Corpl Shaw & 3 men to 12th Brigade for sanitary duties.	
DOMART	"	3 p.m.	Held an examination of the men of my Unit in Sanitation of Battalions.	

Army Form C. 2118

WAR DIARY
or
INTELLIGENCE SUMMARY
(Erase heading not required.)

Instructions regarding War Diaries and Intelligence Summaries are contained in F.S. Regs., Part II. and the Staff Manual respectively. Title Pages will be prepared in manuscript.

Place	Date	Hour	Summary of Events and Information	Remarks and references to Appendices
RUBEAU-COURT	9/11/15	4/30 p.m.	Inspected the Head Quarters 108th Brigade and saw their new system of Sanitary arrangement which they have now completed. Every thing was most Sanitary and in good order.	
Ditto Wierres	13/11/15	10·30 a.m.	Dugouts. Sent Cpl [illeg] & three men of my Unit to the Head Quarters of the 108th Brigade for Sanitary duties.	
BEAUVAL	14/11/15	10·50 a.m.	Sent Sgt Dittrington & three men of my Unit to the Head Quarters of the 109th Brigade for Sanitary duties.	
GEZAIN-COURT	"	12·30 p.m.	Proceeded to Beaumont to disinfect some of the billets of the 9th Royal Irish Fusiliers who had been sent to Hospital with Scabies. Also inspected the Sanitary arrangements of the Regiment which I found on the whole to be good.	
BEAUVAL	"	4 p.m.	Inspected the Sanitary arrangements of the 109th Field Ambulance which were good.	

1875 Wt. W593/826 1,000,000 4/15 J.B.C. & A. A.D'S.S./Forms/C. 2118.

Army Form C. 2118

WAR DIARY
or
INTELLIGENCE SUMMARY
(Erase heading not required.)

Instructions regarding War Diaries and Intelligence Summaries are contained in F.S. Regs., Part II. and the Staff Manual respectively. Title Pages will be prepared in manuscript.

Place	Date	Hour	Summary of Events and Information	Remarks and references to Appendices
DOMART	11/11/15	10-30 a.m.	Gave a demonstration of sanitary matters to the Medical Officers of the 1st King's Own Royal Lancaster Regiment and the 5th South Lancashire Regiment. The Quartermasters of these Regiments were also present.	
"	"	2 p.m.	Superintended the making of a field kitchen for my Unit, in which is incorporated a closed-in hood for disposal of grease waters by evaporation. This is done by heat of fire under the Camp Kettles. It is said by the Sanitary Officers of the 4th Division to be a most excellent way of disposing of grease water, but has not been tried by any before.	
"	12/11/15	10 a.m.	Gave a demonstration to the Medical Officers and Sanitary Sergeants of the 14th Royal Irish Rifles, 11th Royal Irish Rifles and 36th Divisional Train, on Sanitary arrangements for Camps.	

WAR DIARY or INTELLIGENCE SUMMARY

Army Form C. 2118

Place	Date	Hour	Summary of Events and Information	Remarks and references to Appendices
DOMART	12/11/15	11/30 a.m.	Had a fire lighted in its new field kitchen that was made yesterday, combining cooking with evaporation of pisse water by evaporation and found that it answered excellently.	
FLEXA-COURT	13/11/15	3 p.m.	Inspected the Billets and sanitary arrangements of Princess Patricia's Canadian Light Infantry with the ADMS 36th Division. The Billets were good and then let the sanitary arrangements were far from satisfactory. Arranged with the M.O. I/c that he & the sanitary sergeant should come over to DOMART and have a demonstration on sanitary arrangements, results of which I saw at the Billets of my unit, at 3 p.m. tomorrow 13/11/15.	
DOMART	13/11/15	9 a.m.	As the 108th Brigade have been ordered to the trenches, I saw the DADMS 36th Division and arranged with him to write to the Staff Captain 10th Brigade to return the Corporal and 3 men of my unit, who were lent to this Brigade for instructional duties in sanitation.	

Place	Date	Hour	Summary of Events and Information	Remarks and references to Appendices
CANDAS	13/4/15	11 a.m.	Inspected the Billets + saw the sanitary arrangements of the 11th Royal Inniskilling Fusiliers at CANDAS. Billets were clean but the sanitary arrangements were not very satisfactory. Arranged with the M.O i/c to come over tomorrow 14/11/14 to see models of sanitary arrangement. Have made him at Domart	
DOMART	13/4/15	3-30 p.m.	Showed & explained models of sanitary arrangements to the M.O i/c Princess Patricia Canadian Inf 2nd Infantry and also to his Sanitary Sergeant at the Billets of my Unit there.	
ARQUEVES	14/4/15	2 p.m.	Inspected the sanitary arrangements of No 121st Coy R.E. and found them very good in every way.	
DOMART	15/4/15	9 a.m.	A number of Blankets came in from the 100th Field Ambulance to be disinfected. The ambulance was disinfected before returning	
"	"	12 p.m.	Inspected the Divisional Prison and found everything correct	

Army Form C. 2118

WAR DIARY
or
INTELLIGENCE SUMMARY

(Erase heading not required.)

Instructions regarding War Diaries and Intelligence Summaries are contained in F. S. Regs., Part II. and the Staff Manual respectively. Title Pages will be prepared in manuscript.

Place	Date	Hour	Summary of Events and Information	Remarks and references to Appendices
DOMART	16/11/15	9 a.m.	A number of men kits from the 108th Field Ambulance were sent to me to be disinfected. The ambulance was disinfected before sending back.	
DOMART	17/11/15	9 a.m.	Was called on by the A.P.M. to visit a Sergeant of the Kings own who had arrived for duty the night before. I found him under the influence of drink and wrote a report to this effect.	
"	"	10 a.m.	Visited the Divisional Head Quarter Billets and saw the sanitary arrangements which were in good order.	
DOMART	18/11/15	8 a.m.	Sent the motor lorry to collect 100 blankets for disinfection from the 1/4 London Brigade R.F.A. at BONNEVILLE. The motor lorry was disinfected on returning.	
EPECAMPS	"	11 a.m.	Visited the billets and saw the sanitary arrangements of the French Nurses Battalion & found everything correct.	
DOMART	19/11/15	8 a.m.	Sent the motor lorry to collect another 100 blankets for disinfection from the 1/4 London Brigade R.F.A. at BONNEVILLE. The motor lorry was disinfected on returning.	

WAR DIARY
or
INTELLIGENCE SUMMARY

(Erase heading not required.)

Army Form C. 2118

Place	Date	Hour	Summary of Events and Information	Remarks and references to Appendices
RANCHEVAL	28/1/15	11.15 a.m.	Visited the B.Hdts. and saw the Sanitary arrangements of the 16th Royal Irish Rifles at RANCHEVAL. The billets were excellent. Its means for bathing the men were good and its Sanitary arrangements - the onely point the only thing one could find fault with was that the incinerators were not built up to the standard pattern.	
S.Leger	29/1/15	11.30 a.m.	Attended at the Maine S.t LEGER to give evidence against Sgt - at Rens Royal Irish Regiment, for being drunk the afternoon of church on the morning of November 17th 1915.	
DOMART	"	8.30 a.m.	Sent the motor lorry, a corporal and 2 men to disinfect some billets of the 9th Royal Innishilling Fusiliers at GEZAINCOURT.	
S.t LEGER	"	12.00 p.m.	Inspected the sanitary arrangements, laundry and bathing houses of the 1st King's Own Royal Lancashire Regiment and found everything in good order	

WAR DIARY
or
INTELLIGENCE SUMMARY
(Erase heading not required.)

Army Form C. 2118

Place	Date	Hour	Summary of Events and Information	Remarks and references to Appendices
DOMART	21/11/15	10-30 a.m.	Visited the Billets of men employed at Division al H.Q. R.A. at DOMART & saw the sanitary arrangement, billets were in good order, with regard to sanitary arrangements, the incinerator was badly built, read a request from Army hours to show them how to build a proper incinerator.	
"	"	11-30 a.m.	Visited the Billets & saw the sanitary arrangements of the 86th Field Co and found all correct.	
DOMART	22/11/15	10 a.m.	Had a number of Mantels and Pits disinfected for the 108th Field Ambulance	
DOMART	23/11/15	9 a.m.	A number of Pits seen to for disinfection by the 108th Field	
ST OMER	"	11 a.m.	Visited the Billets & saw the sanitary arrangements the squadron of Inniskilling Dragoons found all in good order.	

Army Form C. 2118

WAR DIARY
or
INTELLIGENCE SUMMARY
(Erase heading not required.)

Instructions regarding War Diaries and Intelligence Summaries are contained in F.S. Regs., Part II. and the Staff Manual respectively. Title Pages will be prepared in manuscript.

Place	Date	Hour	Summary of Events and Information	Remarks and references to Appendices
DOMART	24/11/15	9 a.m.	Had a number of Blankets sent for disinfection, by the 109th Field Ambulance. This was done & the Blankets returned.	
"	"	11 a.m.	Visited the Fields & saw the Sanitary arrangements of the 36th Signal Coy. Found all in good order.	
VILLERS BOCAGE	25/11/15	11.15 a.m.	Attended the Casualty Clearing Station at VILLERS BOCAGE to give evidence on a Court Martial, held on Pte. McWhirter of the Inniskilling Dragoons. As an irregularity had occurred in the formation no Court Martial was held.	
DOMART	"	2 p.m.	Gave a demonstration in the use of Smoke Helmets to the men of my Unit.	

WAR DIARY
or
INTELLIGENCE SUMMARY
(Erase heading not required.)

Army Form C. 2118

Place	Date	Hour	Summary of Events and Information	Remarks and references to Appendices
DOMART	26/11/15	10 a.m.	Attended Field Service 36th Division to give evidence in relation to Pte McAlister Fusil. Bulkley Drymen.	
"	"	2 p.m.	Saw a demonstration on the use of Smoke Helmets to the men of the 36th Field Ambulance Workshops.	
DOMART	27/11/15	9 a.m.	Having received orders to move to PONT REMY tomorrow Nov 25th at 9 a.m., I proceeded to have all my Vans packed ready for moving.	
DOMART	28/11/15	9 a.m.	Proceeded to PONT REMY with my Unit. The whole of my motor lorry having burst, the lorry was towed to PONT REMY by the 36 Field Ambulance Workshops lorry. PONT REMY was reached at 11 a.m.	

Army Form C. 2118

WAR DIARY
or
INTELLIGENCE SUMMARY
(Erase heading not required.)

Instructions regarding War Diaries and Intelligence Summaries are contained in F.S. Regs., Part II. and the Staff Manual respectively. Title Pages will be prepared in manuscript.

Place	Date	Hour	Summary of Events and Information	Remarks and references to Appendices
Pont REMY	28/11/15	1-30 p.m.	Took Six men of my Unit to the rooms taken over by Bn H.Q. 36th Division with a fatigue party of the Cyclist Section and had the rooms cleaned out and disinfected.	
Pont REMY	29/11/15	9 a.m.	Visited the Chateau with three men of my Unit and cleaned out & disinfected the rooms to be used as offices by the S.O.C. 36th Division.	
"	"	2 p.m.	Visited the Billets of the 36th Field Ambulance Workshops and a latrine which had been left in a filthy condition to be cleaned out & disinfected by the Field Sanitary authorities. Seeing the Liaison Officer on the subject.	
"	30/11/15	10 a.m.	Sent L/Corporal Smith A. of my Unit to Divisional H.Q.'s 13th Corps for duty as Sanitary Corporal to the D.A.D.M.S. 13th Corps	

Army Form C. 2118

WAR DIARY
or
INTELLIGENCE SUMMARY
(Erase heading not required.)

Instructions regarding War Diaries and Intelligence Summaries are contained in F.S. Regs., Part II. and the Staff Manual respectively. Title Pages will be prepared in manuscript.

Place	Date	Hour	Summary of Events and Information	Remarks and references to Appendices
PONT REMY	3/11/15	11 a.m.	Visited the R.O. Head Quarters at FRANCIERES and saw the Brigade Major with regard to sending him from my Unit to act as adviser to the R.O. Brigade on Sanitary matters. Arranged to send him over (common Dec 1st 1915 at 10 o'clock.	
PONT REMY	"	2 p.m.	Vermin Larvin been seen at H.Q. Offices 36th Division Insect. Cleans to investigate and arranged for the proper kit to shipped from Portsall, also that a Cloak should be supplied of recement and cloak against Vermin of Troops.	

1875 Wt. W593/826 1,000,000 4/15 J.B.C. & A. A.D.S.S./Forms/C. 2118.

mummified but not ablid

10. 76 Jan. Pest.

WAR DIARY
or
INTELLIGENCE SUMMARY
(Erase heading not required.)

Army Form C. 2118

Place	Date	Hour	Summary of Events and Information	Remarks and references to Appendices
PONT REMY	11/11/15	9 a.m.	Reported to A.D.M.S. 36th Division that a number of Billets in the town were insanitary.	
"	"	10 a.m.	Along with the A.D.M.S. & D.A.D.M.S. 36th Division I visited the Billets of the R.H.P. & Pioneers men. Its billets & Pioneers Rooms were seen to in good condition, but the yard was very dirty, and a closet was found filled with human excrement. 92 yard was ordered to be cleared and the closet emptied & closed for the use of troops. A p[it] upon latrine to be made and urine pit also to an circumstan [?] built.	
"	11	11 a.m.	Visited the Billets & saw the Sanitary arrangements of the 36th Cyclist Coy. Billets were in good condition, also Sanitary arrangements with the exception of the Incineration, which were not properly built. Arranged that these should be altered.	

Army Form C. 2118

WAR DIARY
or
INTELLIGENCE SUMMARY
(Erase heading not required.)

Place	Date	Hour	Summary of Events and Information	Remarks and references to Appendices
PONT REMY	1/10/15	12 p.m.	Visited the Reception Room which we saw in good condition, arranged & saw the yard cleaned up.	
LONGUE	11	2 p.m.	Visited the Billets & saw the Sanitary arrangements of the 153rd Field Artillery at LONGUE. The billets were very scrappy, arranged with the Sanitary arrangements were very scrappy. Arranged that the Lodhi should be brought up to the required standard of the Division. The ADMS 36th Division accompanied me.	
CONQUE-REL	2/11/15	3 p.m.	Visited the Billets & advised on the Sanitation of the Ammunition Column of the 153rd Brigade RFA at CONQUEREL with the ADMS 36th Division.	

WAR DIARY
or
INTELLIGENCE SUMMARY
(Erase heading not required.)

Army Form C. 2118

Place	Date	Hour	Summary of Events and Information	Remarks and references to Appendices
Pont Remy	3/12/15	9 a.m.	Inspected an Incinerator which is being built behind the A.D.M.S. office 36th Division, and arranged for a latrine to be erected for men working in the office.	
"	"	11 a.m.	Inspected the models of sanitary appliances which are being built by my Unit.	
LONGUET	"	2 pm	Inspected the billets & sanitary arrangements of D. Battery 153 Brigade R.F.A. which has been transferred to LONGUE	
BOUCHON	4/12/15	9.30 a.m.	Inspected the billets & saw the Sanitary Arrangements of the 172nd Brigade R.F.A. at Bouchon, a large expanse of my Unit was instructing them in the method of building Sanitary appliances.	
COCQUE-REL	"	11-45 a.m.	Visited the Billets of the 154th & 12th Brigade R.F.A. at COCQUEREL & advised the O.11 in regard to Sanitary arrangements. This Battery hospital arrived	

Army Form C. 2118

WAR DIARY
or
INTELLIGENCE SUMMARY
(Erase heading not required.)

Instructions regarding War Diaries and Intelligence Summaries are contained in F.S. Regs., Part II. and the Staff Manual respectively. Title Pages will be prepared in manuscript.

Place	Date	Hour	Summary of Events and Information	Remarks and references to Appendices
PopREMY	4/10/18	2 p.m.	Visited the models of the Sanitary Section 36th Division and arranged a new pattern of field kitchen to be built.	
PopRemy	5/10/18	9 a.m.	Saw the new field kitchen which has been built and arranged for the bed today; also a hand latrine to be built.	
MOUFLIERS	"	11.30 a.m.	Visited the 48th Public Health Veterinary Section + saw the Billets and Sanitary Arrangements. - B.N.T. men in + billets condition.	
"	"	1.30 p.m.	Visited the Billets taken over the Sanitary Arrangements of the 121st Coy RE at MOUFLIERS. Found everything in good condition.	
PopREMY	"	3.30 p.m.	Gave orders for a field kitchen to be built at the Billets of the 76th Sanitary Section, of the same pattern, this was done + is working.	

WAR DIARY
or
INTELLIGENCE SUMMARY
(Erase heading not required.)

Army Form C. 2118

Instructions regarding War Diaries and Intelligence Summaries are contained in F.S. Regs., Part II. and the Staff Manual respectively. Title Pages will be prepared in manuscript.

Place	Date	Hour	Summary of Events and Information	Remarks and references to Appendices
PONT REMY	6/11/15	9 a.m.	Gave orders for a covered latrine to be made as a model. This latrine is to be made of hurdwood & roofed with straw.	
LONG	"	11 a.m.	Visited the billets and saw the Sanitary Arrangements of the 172nd Brigade R.F.A. at LONG. Advised the M.O. i/c with regard to his Sanitary arrangements.	
PONT REMY	"	9 a.m.	Inspected the new latrine built at Bushment. Inspected the mobile of Sanitary appliances built by the 76th Sanitary Section.	
VAUCH-ELLES	14/11/15	11 a.m.	Visited the Billets and saw the Sanitary Arrangements of the 173rd Brigade R.F.A. at VAUCHELLES. Advised the M.O. i/c on Sanitary arrangements.	

Army Form C. 2118

WAR DIARY
or
INTELLIGENCE SUMMARY
(Erase heading not required.)

Instructions regarding War Diaries and Intelligence Summaries are contained in F. S. Regs., Part II. and the Staff Manual respectively. Title Pages will be prepared in manuscript.

Place	Date	Hour	Summary of Events and Information	Remarks and references to Appendices
Puchevillers	8/10/15	"	Getting to report.	
"	9/10/15	11 am	Had Medical Inspection of the F.A.W.U. 36th Division.	
"	"	11.30	Medical Inspection of the 76th Sanitary Section.	
LONGUET	10/10/15	"	Saw the Billets of the 158th Brigade R.F.A. Inckspring.	
LONGUET	11/10/15	12 pm	Inspected Billets of D. Battery 153rd Brigade R.F.A. Inckspring.	
VAUCH-ELLES.	12/10/15	2 pm	Saw the Billets & Sanitary arrangements of the 173rd Brigade R.F.A. at VAUCHELLES. Inckspring.	

WAR DIARY
or
INTELLIGENCE SUMMARY

Army Form C. 2118

Place	Date	Hour	Summary of Events and Information	Remarks and references to Appendices
Pont Remy	13/7/15	9 a.m.	Arranged to run motors & sanitary appliances remote as for as field kitchens & current furnished are concerned.	
"	14/7/15	10 a.m.	Visited billets of R.E. and saw new beds made for men and saw patter of stove for billets.	
"	15/7/15	10 a.m.	Visited H.Q. billets saw sanitary arrangements, satisfactory.	
"	16/7/15	11 a.m.	Visited billets & saw sanitary arrangements of 109th Field Ambulance everything in good order.	
"	17/7/15		Anthony Bowlby	

Army Form C. 2118

WAR DIARY
or
INTELLIGENCE SUMMARY
(Erase heading not required.)

Instructions regarding War Diaries and Intelligence Summaries are contained in F. S. Regs., Part II. and the Staff Manual respectively. Title Pages will be prepared in manuscript.

Place	Date	Hour	Summary of Events and Information	Remarks and references to Appendices
Port Remy	18/1/16	10 a.m.	Visited billets in town of Gyberk & R.E. and found everything satisfactory.	
CONQUE= REU	19/1/16	10 a.m.	Visited Billets & saw Sanitary arrangements of Ammn Column of 153rd R.F.A. Brigade. Arranged for more Incinerators built.	
Beauchen	20/1/16	10 a.m.	Saw billets and Sanitary arrangements of 172nd Brigade R.F.A. Their Sanitary arrangements are in a bad state.	
Port Remy	21/1/16	11 a.m.	Inspected the billets of 76th Sanitary Section & saw 36 nDivision and all medical Supplies & kits, satisfactory.	
Port Remy	22/1/16	6 a.m.	Went on leave to England to 4th January 1916.	

1875 Wt. W593/826 1,000,000 4/15 J.B.C. & A. A.D.S.S./Forms/C. 2118.

36

76 Sam Sect
36th Div

Vol. 3

36th Div

Jan/1916
to
Dec 1916

Army Form C. 2118

WAR DIARY
or
INTELLIGENCE SUMMARY
(Erase heading not required.)

Instructions regarding War Diaries and Intelligence Summaries are contained in F. S. Regs., Part II. and the Staff Manual respectively. Title Pages will be prepared in manuscript.

Place	Date	Hour	Summary of Events and Information	Remarks and references to Appendices
DOMART	5/11/16	8 p.m.	Arrived DOMART from leave.	
"	6/11/16	9 a.m.	Inspected billets of 76 Sanitary Section and arranged for proper sanitary arrangements to be made.	
"	"	1 p.m.	Arranged for proper latrine to be made at office of ADMS and to inspect the billets.	
"	"	2 p.m.	Inspected Billets of S.A.N.U. Schezpedery	
"	7/11/16	9 a.m.	Wrote to report.	
"	8/11/16	9 a.m.	Inspected billets of HQ troops. Schezpedery.	
St HILAIRE	"	11 a.m.	Visited billets to an Sanitary arrangements of 36th Service Squadron from Rothrey Dragons at St HILAIRE, Schezpedery.	

WAR DIARY
or
INTELLIGENCE SUMMARY
(Erase heading not required.)

Army Form C. 2118

Instructions regarding War Diaries and Intelligence Summaries are contained in F. S. Regs., Part II. and the Staff Manual respectively. Title Pages will be prepared in manuscript.

Place	Date	Hour	Summary of Events and Information	Remarks and references to Appendices
CANAPLES	9/1/16	11 a.m.	Inspected billets & saw Sanitary arrangements of 11th Royal Irish Rifles at CANAPLES. Sanitary arrangements might be improved. Saw M.O. i/c re Trephyle.	
BERNEUIL	10/1/16	10 a.m.	Inspected the billets & saw Sanitary arrangements of 14th F.P. of R.d. BERNEUIL. Schofeuding.	
DOMART	11/1/16	9 a.m.	Inspected billets & saw Sanitary arrangements of Div. Cyclist Coy. Schofeuding.	
"	"	11 a.m.	Inspected billets & Sanitary arrangements of 36th Signal Coy. Schofeuding.	
"	"	2 p.m.	Inspected billets and saw Sanitary arrangements of F A W V 36th Div Schofeuding.	

Army Form C. 2118

WAR DIARY
or
INTELLIGENCE SUMMARY
(Erase heading not required.)

Instructions regarding War Diaries and Intelligence Summaries are contained in F.S. Regs., Part II. and the Staff Manual respectively. Title Pages will be prepared in manuscript.

Place	Date	Hour	Summary of Events and Information	Remarks and references to Appendices
CANDAS	12/1/16	11 a.m.	Inspected billets and sanitary arrangements of 16th R.I.R. at CANDAS. Schutzheim.	
RIBEAU-COURT	13/1/16	10 a.m.	Inspected HQ billets & sanitation of 108th Brigade at RIBEAUCOURT Schutzheim.	
"	"	11-30 a.m.	Inspected billets & sanitary arrangements of 12th R.I.R. at RIBEAUCOURT, Schutzheim.	
BEAU-METZ	14/1/16	11 a.m.	Inspected billets & sanitary arrangements of 13th R.I.R. at BEAUMETZ, billets with Regt billets. Saw I.O.C. and arranged for the latrines.	
DOMART	15/1/16	9 a.m.	Dispatched a number of blankets for 105th Field Ambulance.	
"	"	11 a.m.	Inspected H.Q. billets. Signed Capt's billet - Schutzheim	

Army Form C. 2118

WAR DIARY
or
INTELLIGENCE SUMMARY
(Erase heading not required.)

Instructions regarding War Diaries and Intelligence Summaries are contained in F. S. Regs., Part II. and the Staff Manual respectively. Title Pages will be prepared in manuscript.

Place	Date	Hour	Summary of Events and Information	Remarks and references to Appendices
MONTRE-LET	16/11/16	10 a.m.	Inspected billets & sanitary arrangements of H Q Divisional Train at MONTRELET, satisfactory.	
DOMART	17/11/16	9 a.m.	76th Sanitary Section known to BERNAVILLE tomorrow, had 2 disinfectors taken down and stores packed as far as possible.	
DOMART	18/11/16	9 a.m.	Left DOMART for BERNAVILLE with 86th FAWC	
BERNA-VILLE	"	2 p.m.	Took over billets for men of 76th Sanitary Section.	
BERNA-VILLE	19/11/16	9 a.m.	Inspected billets & sanitary arrangements of HQ billets at BERNAVILLE, arranged to have new urinals built.	
"	"	11-30 a.m.	Inspected billets & sanitary arrangements of 36th Lt. what Coys, satisfactory	

Army Form C. 2118

WAR DIARY
or
INTELLIGENCE SUMMARY
(Erase heading not required.)

Instructions regarding War Diaries and Intelligence Summaries are contained in F.S. Regs., Part II. and the Staff Manual respectively. Title Pages will be prepared in manuscript.

Place	Date	Hour	Summary of Events and Information	Remarks and references to Appendices
CANDAS	20/1/16	10·30 a.m.	Inspected billets & sanitary arrangements of 16th R.I.R. at CANDAS. Satisfactory.	
FIEN-VILLERS	"	2 p.m.	Inspected billets & saw Sanitary arrangements of HQ 109th Brigade at FIENVILLERS. Satisfactory.	
"	21/1/16	10 a.m.	Inspected billet & sanitary arrangements of 9th Royal Inniskillings at FIENVILLERS. Billets — yards of billets pointed out to officer concerned, arranged with 2 O/C to have bins there.	
BEAU-METZ	22/1/16	11 a.m.	Inspected billets — Sanitary arrangements of 13th R.O.R. at BEAUMETZ. Satisfactory.	
PROU-VILLE	23/1/16	11·30 a.m.	Inspected billets & sanitary arrangements of 9th Royal Irish Fusiliers at PROUVILLE. Satisfactory.	

WAR DIARY
or
INTELLIGENCE SUMMARY

(Erase heading not required.)

Army Form C. 2118

Place	Date	Hour	Summary of Events and Information	Remarks and references to Appendices
BERNA-VILLE	24/1/16	6 a.m.	Inspected billets of H.Q, 36th Cy Lit Coy & FAWU and found everything satisfactory.	
DOMES-MONT	25/1/16	10 a.m.	Inspected billets & saw Sanitary arrangements of 121st Coy R.E. at DOMESMONT, satisfactory.	
ST OUEN	26/1/16	11 a.m.	Inspected billets & saw Sanitary arrangements of 36th Div Amm Column at ST OUEN, very satisfactory.	
EPE-CAMPS	27/1/16	12 p.m.	Visited HQ 36th Fifld Cy and Div I Cy at EPECAMPS, billets - also hspl cleans also kitchens, saw O.C. who arranged to move the three.	

Army Form C. 2118

WAR DIARY
or
INTELLIGENCE SUMMARY
(Erase heading not required.)

Instructions regarding War Diaries and Intelligence Summaries are contained in F. S. Regs., Part II. and the Staff Manual respectively. Title Pages will be prepared in manuscript.

Place	Date	Hour	Summary of Events and Information	Remarks and references to Appendices
RIBEAU-COURT	29/1/16	10-30 a.m.	Inspected billets and Sanitary arrangements of H.Q. 105th Brigade at RIBEAUCOURT, Sub Jarking	
"	"	12 p.m.	Inspected billets of 12th R.D.F. at RIBEAUCOURT, Sub Jarking	
BERTEAU COURT	29/1/16	11 a.m.	Inspected billets and Sanitary arrangements of 109th Field Ambulance at BERTEAU COURT, Sub Jarking.	
CANDAS	30/1/16	11 a.m.	Visited billets and Sanitary arrangements of 45th Field Veterinary Section at CANDAS, Sub Jarking.	
VACQUE-RIE	31/1/16	10 a.m.	Inspected billets and Sanitary arrangements of 105th Field Ambulance at VACQUERIE, Sub Jarking.	

1875 Wt. W593/826 1,000,000 4/15 J.B.C. &A. A.D.S.S./Forms/C. 2118.

Army Form C. 2118

WAR DIARY
or
INTELLIGENCE SUMMARY

(Erase heading not required.)

Instructions regarding War Diaries and Intelligence Summaries are contained in F. S. Regs., Part II. and the Staff Manual respectively. Title Pages will be prepared in manuscript.

Place	Date	Hour	Summary of Events and Information	Remarks and references to Appendices
ACHEUX	7/2/16	9 a.m.	Moved from BERNAVILLE with Field Ambulance to take up Unit Convoy with my lorry.	
"	"	12-30 p.m.	Arrived at ACHEUX and took over Billet No 66 for my men. A/l, dinner men of my Unit cleared out billet & yard, put up latrine in an outhouse, built a field kitchen and dug a urine pit.	
ACHEUX	8/2/16	8 a.m.	Started to build an incinerator for disposal of rubbish & excreta at my Billet. Had billets thoroughly washed out and disinfected.	
"	"	1/30 p.m.	Incinerator finished, built new latrin field kitchen for cooking boiling water and disposal of greasy water by evaporation.	
"	9/2/16	8-30 a.m.	Built an incinerator at 1st Hrs Quarter Billets for destruction of rubbish & excreta.	
"	"	1-30 p.m.	Had a fifteen urine pit dug & filled with burnt tin cans and stones.	

WAR DIARY
or
INTELLIGENCE SUMMARY

(Erase heading not required.)

Army Form C. 2118

Place	Date	Hour	Summary of Events and Information	Remarks and references to Appendices
ACHEUX	9/4/15	10 a.m.	Visited Sucherie at ACHEUX. Inspected water supply and took samples of water, arranged with the Senr Commandant to have the whole of the ground round the Sucherie cleared up, and to have three incinerators built at three different places, one near the Boilers, one near the cookhouse stove and one in the main yard, for the destruction of rubbish and excreta. Place to be the same covered in pattern.	
"	"	12/15 p.m.	Saw the Staff Capt'n 109th Brigade and arranged that the four men of my Unit should be relieved from tomorrow for duty, from this Brigade.	
LEAVILLERS	"	1-30 p.m.	Sent two men to disinfect a Billet for 9th / Eng. A.S.C. at LEAVILLERS.	
ACHEUX	"	2-30 p.m.	Ten men from the 36th Cyclist Coy reported to me for duty with the Sanitary Section.	

WAR DIARY
or
INTELLIGENCE SUMMARY

Army Form C. 2118

Place	Date	Hour	Summary of Events and Information	Remarks and references to Appendices
QCHEUX	10/2/16	9.30 a.m.	Visited H.Q. Billets and found Serviceton and Uxevington finished and in watering order, inspected the Billets and found them satisfactory.	
"	"	11 a.m.	Visited Suchin and found that old method are executed softly the last Division had been turned in instead.	
"	"	2 p.	Had an inspection properly built, a soak pit dug, and the yard cleaned up of the Head Quarter Staff working at the School House.	
"	"	4 p.	Had a soak pit dug filled in for my attestors shed at my mens billet.	
"	"	2 p.	Sent Corporal Sloan of my unit to the 121st Coy R.E. at FORCEVILLE to shew them how to erect a new pattern field kitchen	

Army Form C. 2118

WAR DIARY
or
INTELLIGENCE SUMMARY
(Erase heading not required.)

Instructions regarding War Diaries and Intelligence Summaries are contained in F. S. Regs., Part II. and the Staff Manual respectively. Title Pages will be prepared in manuscript.

Place	Date	Hour	Summary of Events and Information	Remarks and references to Appendices
ACHEUX	11/2/16	8 am	Had lorry pit dug & filled in for Signal Coy RE & ADMS' Office. Started to build new petrol driveries for Staff Officers.	
"	"	10 am	Visited Suchries at ACHEUX and inspected billets, latrines and saw the sanitary arrangements of Army Ordnance Admin. Latrines & billets very dirty, spoke to O.C., who promised to have this remedied at once.	
"	"	11 am	Visited Field Force Canteen and ordered all rubbish lying about outside the store to be burnt at once.	
"	"	11/30 am	Visited Billets of 4th Division Ammunition Column and found the yard dirty, ordered it to be cleared.	
"	"	12/15 pm	Visited Billets of the 36th Division Signal Coy and reported to O.C. that the yards & billets of this unit required attention. They were far from clean. He ordered the late home.	

1875 Wt. W593/826 1,000,000 4/15 J.B.C. & A. A.D.S.S./Forms/C. 2118.

WAR DIARY
or
INTELLIGENCE SUMMARY
(Erase heading not required.)

Army Form C. 2118

Place	Date	Hour	Summary of Events and Information	Remarks and references to Appendices
ACHEUX	10/2/16	2.30 p.m.	Visited Billets and saw the Sanitary Arrangements of the 109th R.E. Railway Dumps and found them satisfactory.	
"	"	3.30 p.m.	Visited 15th Res of R.E. Head Quarter Clerks at Billet No 70, ordered 15th Res Room to be cleaned out, then being dirty.	
"	11/2/16	8 a.m.	Sent two complete box disinfectors to the 110th Field Ambulance by order of the A.D.M.S. 36th Division.	
"	"	9 a.m.	Started to build a new pattern Field Kitchen at H.Q. Billets for cooking food, trying 10 gallons of milk in two oil drums, and disposal of greasy waste by evaporation.	
"	"	9.30 a.m.	Look over Billet No 67 for the men of the 36th Division by shot [?] my who are attached to army unit for duty.	

WAR DIARY
or
INTELLIGENCE SUMMARY
(Erase heading not required.)

Army Form C. 2118

Place	Date	Hour	Summary of Events and Information	Remarks and references to Appendices
ACHEUX	19/2/16	11 a.m.	Returned 9 tin tins of biscuits and several crates of bivouac huts to A.S.C. at FORCEVILLERS which were found to be spare if any more Billets to our arrival at ACHEUX.	
"	"	2 p.m.	Had a Latrine built and a 4 upper urine pit to made out 175 Great Division for the English Soldiers employed here.	
"	"	3 p.m.	Orders received from A.D.M.S. 36th Division for me to see the Sick at H.Q. Medical Enquire Room daily as a temporary measure.	
"	"	3-30 p.m.	Wrote to C.R.E. 36th Division asking that I might have huts with which to build Lavoratories & Field Kitchens.	
"	"	4 p.m.	Inspected billet house of H.Q. Unit and found every Reny Satisfactory	

WAR DIARY
or
INTELLIGENCE SUMMARY

(Erase heading not required.)

Army Form C. 2118

Instructions regarding War Diaries and Intelligence Summaries are contained in F. S. Regs., Part II. and the Staff Manual respectively. Title Pages will be prepared in manuscript.

Place	Date	Hour	Summary of Events and Information	Remarks and references to Appendices
ACHEUX	13/2/16	10 a.m.	Inspected Field Kitchen being built at Head Quarters. Billets by over ½ the 76th Sanitary Section.	
"	"	11 a.m.	Inspected the Military Police Billets and saw their Sanitary arrangements. Found billets clean and sanitary arrangements satisfactory.	
"	"	2 p.m.	Inspected the Billets of the 45½ Mobile Veterinary Section and found them clean. Appears incinerator should be built and also a proper urine pit. Saw the C.O. & arranged for this to be done.	
"	"	4 p.m.	Saw Town Commandant re yards at Station ACHEUX. The yards wants cleaning up, arranged with him to have it done.	

Army Form C. 2118

WAR DIARY
or
INTELLIGENCE SUMMARY

(Erase heading not required.)

Instructions regarding War Diaries and Intelligence Summaries are contained in F.S. Regs., Part II. and the Staff Manual respectively. Title Pages will be prepared in manuscript.

Place	Date	Hour	Summary of Events and Information	Remarks and references to Appendices
ACHEUX	14/2/16	9 a.m.	Sent a Corporal of my Unit to 4 & 5th Mobile Vet Section to instruct this section how to build an Incinerator according to pattern	
"	"	10 a.m.	Inspected Incinerator building at the Suchewie ACH EUX. Gave instructions how the built line, arranged that paper wire pits be built line also.	
"	"	2 p.m.	Inspected Billets of H.Q. R.E., also Post Office R.E. Billets – issued cleaning up as do their Stables, saw the Adjutant on the subject who promised to see the attached to Billets at Post Office were clean.	

1875 Wt. W593/826 1,000,000 4/15 J.B.C. & A. A.D.S.S./Forms/C. 2118.

Place	Date	Hour	Summary of Events and Information	Remarks and references to Appendices
ACHEUX	15/7/16	10 a.m.	Saw two incinerators which have been built in regards at Suchenis ACHEUX and arranged for a third to be built. Arranged for pits to be dug for their incinerators.	
"	"	11.30 p.m	Inspected billets of R.F.A. at ACHEUX and found them correct and their sanitary arrangements satisfactory.	
"	"	2 p.m	Arranged with D.A.D.M.S. 36th Division to billet 12 Rifle Bgde. employed at the Baths, in the Billets of my Unit.	
"	"	4 p.m.	Inspected H.Q. billets and saw their sanitary arrangements found it correct.	

Army Form C. 2118

WAR DIARY
or
INTELLIGENCE SUMMARY
(Erase heading not required.)

Place	Date	Hour	Summary of Events and Information	Remarks and references to Appendices
ACHEUX	10/2/16	10 a.m.	Inspected H.Q. R.A. Found latrine buckets had not been emptied regularly, arranged with Staff Captain that this should be done.	
"	"	11 a.m.	Inspected sanitary arrangements of Y.M.C.A. arranged Kean as incinerator built for burning excreta & rubbish.	
"	"	2 p.m.	Sent six of my Unit as sanitary inspectors to six Town Commandants in the Divisional Area.	
"	"	5 p.m.	Lieut Craig O.C. F.A.W.V. 36th Division reported to me an instructions proceeded to LEALVILLERS. Arranged to inspect it tomorrow morning	

WAR DIARY
or
INTELLIGENCE SUMMARY
(Erase heading not required.)

Army Form C. 2118

Instructions regarding War Diaries and Intelligence Summaries are contained in F. S. Regs., Part II. and the Staff Manual respectively. Title Pages will be prepared in manuscript.

Place	Date	Hour	Summary of Events and Information	Remarks and references to Appendices
LEAL-VILLERS	17/9/16	10 a.m.	Inspected insanitary pond near Billets of No 3 Coy ASC at LEALVILLERS and advised it should be drained into a properly made soak pit & & some stones + then filled in.	
"	"	11 a.m.	Inspected the Billets and saw the sanitary arrangements of the three Coys ASC at LEALVILLERS, found everything in good order.	
"	"	2 p.m.	Inspected Billets and saw sanitary arrangements of 36 Div. F.A.W.V. Billets clean & sanitary arrangements just er of an incinerator wants building for these billets.	
"	"	4 p.m.	Inspected an Field Oven just built by men of the Sanitary section at HQ billets. Found it working well.	

Army Form C. 2118

WAR DIARY
or
INTELLIGENCE SUMMARY
(Erase heading not required.)

Place	Date	Hour	Summary of Events and Information	Remarks and references to Appendices
FORCE-VILLE	18/2/16	10 a.m.	Inspected billets & saw Sanitary arrangements of 9th R.I.R. and 10th R.I.R. at FORCEVILLE, found billets & yards dirty, reported to Town Commandant.	
"	"	11 a.m.	Inspected Billets & saw Sanitary arrangements of Labour Battalion stationed at FORCEVILLE. Found everything in good order.	
"	"	11/30 a.m.	Inspected Billets & saw Sanitary arrangements of 11th Royal Innniskilling Fusiliers at FORCEVILLE, billets were dirty & sanitary arrangements far from satisfactory, saw Town Commandant who arranged to have them cleaned.	
"	"	2 p.m.	Saw Sanitary arrangements and inspected billets of Pte 121st Coy R.E. and found everything correct.	

Army Form C. 2118

WAR DIARY
or
INTELLIGENCE SUMMARY
(Erase heading not required.)

Place	Date	Hour	Summary of Events and Information	Remarks and references to Appendices
ACHEUX	19/2/16	9 am	Saw Town Commandant who consulted me as to the general sanitation of the Town of ACHEUX	
"	"	11 am	Saw M.O. 1/c Baths and requested him to hasten up the Blankets for the 10th Batt Royal Inniskilling Fusiliers in his Ghost Disinfector.	
"	"	2 pm	Had drains deepened all round Y.M.C.A. to take away scum & wash as there was still cess-pit full.	
FORCE-VILLE	"	3 pm	Inspected rer huts. Saw Sanitary arrangements of 11th Oxon Cavalry Corps & Stewarts Smokes Kitchens at FORCEVILLE, all in good order, but incinerators burnt to trellis to turn intricate & executor. Arranged with the two M.O's that the should be done.	

Army Form C. 2118

WAR DIARY
or
INTELLIGENCE SUMMARY
(Erase heading not required.)

Place	Date	Hour	Summary of Events and Information	Remarks and references to Appendices
ACHEUX	20/2/16	9 am	Inspected motor, made for my truck, and los field kitchen in yard of my billet repaired.	
"	"	10 am	Inspected Baths at Sucrerie and saw the Sanitary arrangements for the same, found all in good order.	
"	"	11 am	Inspected Billets of A.O.D. and R.E. at Sucrerie ACHEUX. Then sent to put & clean, arranged with Officers in charge to have this done. Re Yard at Sucrerie went clothing up regularly, arranged for Inn Commandant to run a fatigue party to the this daily.	
"	"	2 pm	Had the yard of my Billets filled in with chalk stones	
"	"	3 pm	D.A.D.S. 86th Division inspected billets of 76th Sanitary Section & found everything correct.	

Army Form C. 2118

Instructions regarding War Diaries and Intelligence Summaries are contained in F. S. Regs., Part II. and the Staff Manual respectively. Title Pages will be prepared in manuscript.

WAR DIARY
or
INTELLIGENCE SUMMARY
(Erase heading not required.)

Place	Date	Hour	Summary of Events and Information	Remarks and references to Appendices
ACHEUX	2/12/16	9 a.m.	Arranged with O.C. Signals to build a field Kitchen for his men behind his office.	
VARENNES	11	11 a.m.	Inspected 14th Royal Irish Rifles at VARENNES and found all correct.	
"	11	12 p.m.	Inspected Cyclist Coy at VARENNES & found all correct.	
ACHEUX	11	2 p.m.	Allotted Incinerator behind A.D.M.S. Office from an open to a closed one, in order that excreta as well as Refuse may be burnt.	

1875 Wt. W593/826 1,000,000 4/15 J.B.C. & A. A.D.S.S./Forms/C. 2118.

Place	Date	Hour	Summary of Events and Information	Remarks and references to Appendices
ACHEUX	22/2/16	10 a.m.	Inspected Kitchen & sanitary arrangements of HQ Divn No 2. Yard. Should be cleaner & a proper incinerator built, also arn grease pit. Saw officer in charge who is making arrangements about this matter.	
"	"	11 a.m.	Inspected R.A. billets of 32nd Division stationed in ACHEUX. Latrine buckets should be emptied regularly and an old cart chosen — told them. Arranged for this to be done.	
"	"	12 p.m.	Inspected billets of R.G.A. in ACHEUX, billets for horses and a proper cook house. I had to wait. Saw O.C. and arranged for this to be done.	
"	"	2 p.m.	As yard of the 14th Ammunition Column required cleaning up, saw the farm commandant & arranged for this being done.	

WAR DIARY
or
INTELLIGENCE SUMMARY

(Erase heading not required.)

Army Form C. 2118

Instructions regarding War Diaries and Intelligence Summaries are contained in F.S. Regs., Part II. and the Staff Manual respectively. Title Pages will be prepared in manuscript.

Place	Date	Hour	Summary of Events and Information	Remarks and references to Appendices
ACHEUX	23/7/16	9 a.m.	Had Dr Yard to my billets - cleared out and posted orders with chalk Notices, also had incinerators repaired.	
"	"	11 a.m.	Inspected all billets - occupied by men of a attached for duty with the A.O.D. in ACHEUX. General plan is good order.	
"	"	2 p.m.	Saw M.O. He Batts with regard to leaving a number of Markets disinfected.	
"	24/7/16	9 a.m. to 10 a.m.	Inspected all billets and saw the sanitary arrangements of all Troops in ACHEUX not Leaving a N.C.O attached with the Town Commandant.	

1875 Wt. W593/826 1,000,000 4/15 J.B.C. & A. A.D.S.S./Forms/C. 2118.

Army Form C. 2118

WAR DIARY
or
INTELLIGENCE SUMMARY
(Erase heading not required.)

Instructions regarding War Diaries and Intelligence Summaries are contained in F. S. Regs., Part II. and the Staff Manual respectively. Title Pages will be prepared in manuscript.

Place	Date	Hour	Summary of Events and Information	Remarks and references to Appendices
ACHEUX	25/6/16	9 am	Sent to O.C. 121st Coy R.E. at FORCEVILLE for timber & nails to enable some huts for men of my units to obtain littles	
CLAIR-FAYE	"	11 am	Visited and inspected the sanitary arrangements of the 110th Field Ambulance at CLAIRFAYE and found everything in good order.	
ACHEUX	27/2/16	11 am	Inspected the Central Pool of Men of the 36th Div by chit-Corps on the ACHEUX-BERTRANCOURT road, found them in a dirty condition, arranged to have the place disinfected.	
"	"	2 pm	Inspected the billets of the 16th R.I.R. Pioneers in ACHEUX and found things satisfactory.	

WAR DIARY
or
INTELLIGENCE SUMMARY

(Erase heading not required.)

Army Form C. 2118

Place	Date	Hour	Summary of Events and Information	Remarks and references to Appendices
ACHEUX	28/2/16	9 a.m.	Visited Success and inspected all billets, yards and sanitary arrangements there, found things in state which were fairly satisfactory, yards seemed to be fairly cleaner, saw Town Commandant in the matter. A new Drierich be built for the Baths.	
LEALVIL-LERS	"	2 p.m.	Inspected Divisional Train 36th Division, billets arrangements, found everything correct.	
ACHEUX	29/2/16	9-30 a.m.	Inspected the billets just vacated by the 15-12 R.I.R. with the Town Commandant and found things satisfactory.	
"	"	9 a.m.	Men of my unit proceeded to build a new Drierich at the Baths - ACHEUX.	
"	"	2 p.m.	Inspected Corked Post at ACHEUX - FORCEVILLE Road, satisfactory	

WAR DIARIES

of

76th Sanitary Section- for the months of

March and April 1916 — 36th Division —

Confidential

War Diary of Capt J. Davies R.A.M.C,
O.C. 76th Sanitary Section,   76. San Sec
30th Division.   vol. 4

To.   The Officer,
       i/c Adjutant General's Office,
                              Base.

                                    March 1916

WAR DIARY
or
INTELLIGENCE SUMMARY

(Erase heading not required.)

Army Form C. 2118

Place	Date	Hour	Summary of Events and Information	Remarks and references to Appendices
VAUCH-ELLES	1/3/16	10.30 a.m.	Inspected billets & sanitary arrangements of Service Squadron, Dismounted Dragoons, No 5 Entrenching Battalion, and 104th Field Ambulance at VAUCHELLES. Sods Jarling. Arranged to send Cpl McColomb to D.un Commandant of my Unit to D.un Commandant at VAUCHELLES as Sanitary Inspector.	
ACHEUX	2/3/16	9 a.m.	Sent Cpl McColomb for duty with Town Commandant at VADDHELLES.	
FORCE-VILLE	2/2 3/3/16	12/3 6 a.m.	Visited Billets of draught Coy of 11th R.D.R. found billets yards and kitchen very dirty, reported to D.un Commandant who promised to have this insanitary state remedied.	
"	"	2 p.m.	Visited Billets & sanitary arrangements of 121st Coy R.E. at FORCEVILLE. Very sod Jarling.	

WAR DIARY
or
INTELLIGENCE SUMMARY
(Erase heading not required.)

Army Form C. 2118

Place	Date	Hour	Summary of Events and Information	Remarks and references to Appendices
VARENNES	3/3/16	11 a.m.	Visited Billets & Sanitary arrangements of 36th Div Cyclist Coy. Billets clean, sanitary arrangements satisfactory. Grants of latrines daily Pail of camp San Iron convenient. Men exempt from Pass Parade.	
"	"	11.30 a.m.	Visited billets & sanitary arrangements 10th R.I.R. at VARENNES. Satisfactory.	
ACHEUX	4/3/16	9 a.m.	Started to inspect beds of muck & urine for men of Cyclist Coy attached here to dump.	
"	"	"	Owing heavy fall of snow unable to build field urine air-billets of my unit.	

Army Form C. 2118

WAR DIARY
or
INTELLIGENCE SUMMARY
(Erase heading not required.)

Instructions regarding War Diaries and Intelligence Summaries are contained in F. S. Regs., Part II. and the Staff Manual respectively. Title Pages will be prepared in manuscript.

Place	Date	Hour	Summary of Events and Information	Remarks and references to Appendices
ACHEUX	5/9/16	6 a.m.	Privies in watering tubs of Rest Farm in billets 15 & 76 disinfected.	
"	"	4 p.m.	The Germans started a severe shell fire - firing about 30 shells. Men have no exposure they stopped.	
ENGLE-BELMER	6/9/16	10 a.m.	Inspected billets & sanitary arrangements of 9th Royal Irish Fusiliers. Satisfactory.	
"	"	10/30 a.m.	Inspected billets & sanitary arrangements of Coy of 36th Divisional Signal Coy. billets should be cleaner, spoke to OC about it.	
"	"	11 a.m.	Inspected HQ of 10 & 3rd Brigade. Guard room & billets sounded & cleaner. Arranged with J/Sgt Captain & have the latrines.	
"	"	11/30 a.m.	Inspected 10 7th Machine gun Coy's billets & sanitary arrangements. Satisfactory.	

WAR DIARY
or
INTELLIGENCE SUMMARY

(Erase heading not required.)

Army Form C. 2118

Instructions regarding War Diaries and Intelligence Summaries are contained in F.S. Regs., Part II. and the Staff Manual respectively. Title Pages will be prepared in manuscript.

Place	Date	Hour	Summary of Events and Information	Remarks and references to Appendices
ENGLE-BELMER	6/3/16	2 p.m.	Inspected dug-outs & sanitary arrangements of 174th Brigade RFA Schofield.	
"	"	3 p.m.	Inspected billets & saw sanitary arrangements of 13th Royal Irish Rifles Schofield.	
MAILLY MAILLET	7/3/16	10/30 a.m.	Inspected billets & saw sanitary arrangements of 150 Coy R.E. Schofield.	
"	"	12 p.m.	Inspected Bodilis, finish pond, & new hide & is is covered situation, also new mains for the Dumps to under repairs, is now looking very neat & present.	
"	"	2 p.m.	Inspected sanitary arrangements of 8th R.I. Rifles, Schofield.	
"	"	2/30 p.m.	Inspected billets & sanitary arrangements of 9 & R.I. Rifles, Schofield.	

Army Form C. 2118

WAR DIARY
or
INTELLIGENCE SUMMARY
(Erase heading not required.)

Instructions regarding War Diaries and Intelligence Summaries are contained in F. S. Regs., Part II. and the Staff Manual respectively. Title Pages will be prepared in manuscript.

Place	Date	Hour	Summary of Events and Information	Remarks and references to Appendices
MAILLY MAILLET	7/3/16	3/15 p.m	Inspected huts of 4th West Riding Regmt & saw Sanitary arrangements. Gave inspection report, saw Divn Commander on the subject.	
"	"	4 p.m	Saw hts & Sanitary arrangemts of 5th West Riding Regt. T.F. Plan might be changed reinforced upon, saw Divn Commander on the subject.	
"	"	4/30 p.m.	Divnl Regmt of B. Battery 172 Brigade is a very shifty J. Pati., saw adjutant who promised to do it is remedied. Hs. S.S. th Battery - R.F.A., h/r 152 Bde is in a very shifty state. R.F.A.	
ACHEUX	8/3/16	9/15 a.m	A complaint having been received from 36 Divisn of Insane Ho. manure is being piled too near on of their Supply Dumps. Inspected the place on the ACHEUX - LIEVILLERS Road this morning, and	

WAR DIARY
or
INTELLIGENCE SUMMARY
(Erase heading not required.)

Army Form C. 2118

Place	Date	Hour	Summary of Events and Information	Remarks and references to Appendices
ACHEUX	8/3/16	9.30 a.m.	Wrote to HQ 36th Division Q Branch suggesting that as more manure be hoped at the place, that other manure is there be spread over the fields, that a man ist to be chosen for spreading manure.	
LIEL-VILLIERS	"	10/30	Inspected 36th Divisional Canteen at LIEZVILLIERS and found to be very dirty - saw officer in charge and arranged to have same cleaned up.	
"	"	11 a.m.	Inspected HQ 36th Divisional Farm. Satisfactory	
"	"	12 p.m.	Inspected Officers Rest Station. Satisfactory	

Army Form C. 2118

WAR DIARY
or
INTELLIGENCE SUMMARY
(Erase heading not required.)

Instructions regarding War Diaries and Intelligence Summaries are contained in F. S. Regs., Part II. and the Staff Manual respectively. Title Pages will be prepared in manuscript.

Place	Date	Hour	Summary of Events and Information	Remarks and references to Appendices
BERT-RANCOURT	9/3/16	10/30 a.m.	Inspected billets & Sanitary arrangements of 172 Bde and R.F.A. Ammunition Column. Billets satisfactory; yards want cleaning up and manure removing to field and spreading.	
"	"	11/30	Inspected billets & sanitary arrangements of 109th Field Ambulance, satisfactory.	
MAILLY-MAILLET	"	12/30 p.m.	Inspected Sanitary arrangements & Dressing Station of Section of 109th Field Ambulance, satisfactory.	
ACHEUX	10/3/16	9/30 a.m.	Inspected billets of 16th Heavy Artillery R.G.A. and found them in a very dirty condition. Kept left this morning at 4 a.m. reported the matter to the C.O. No.5 36 mg division.	

Army Form C. 2118

WAR DIARY
or
INTELLIGENCE SUMMARY
(Erase heading not required.)

Place	Date	Hour	Summary of Events and Information	Remarks and references to Appendices
ACHEUX	10/3/16	11 a.m.	Inspected Billets & Sanitary arrangements of 48th Trench Mortar Section, Sébastopol.	
"	11/3/16	10 a.m.	Inspected Sanitary arrangements at Sucrerie ACHEUX. Ordnance billets dirty. Also latrine. Reported to O/C who is giving this remedied. Cook house R.A.M.C. van attached to Baths, dirty, reported to O/C who is having it cleaned up. Baths, Sébastopol.	
"	11/3/16	2 p.m.	Saw Town Commandant with regard to order for spending Bonnes for billets in ACHEUX	

Army Form C. 2118

WAR DIARY
or
INTELLIGENCE SUMMARY

(Erase heading not required.)

Instructions regarding War Diaries and Intelligence Summaries are contained in F. S. Regs, Part II. and the Staff Manual respectively. Title Pages will be prepared in manuscript.

Place	Date	Hour	Summary of Events and Information	Remarks and references to Appendices
MAILLY MAILLET	12/9/16	11 a.m.	Visited HWks of 4th & 5th West Riding Regiments at MAILLY — MAILLET. Satisfactory.	
ARQUE-VES.	19/9/16	10/30 a.m.	Inspected HWks & Sanitary arrangements of the Divisional Ammunition Column at ARQUEVES, Satisfactory.	
"	"	12 p.m.	Inspected HWks & saw sanitary arrangements of 1/4 King's Own Yorkshire L.I. at Depot, Satisfactory.	
"	"	12/45 p.m.	Inspected HWks & saw arrangements of 2nd Labour Battalion. Satisfactory.	
LEAL-VILLERS	"	2/30 p.m.	Inspected HWks & saw sanitary arrangements of No 3 Coy, Divisional Train, A.S.C. most excellent.	
"	"	4 p.m.	Inspected HWks & organization of Field Ambulance was a less their very front in every respect.	

1875 Wt. W593/826 1,000,000 4/15 J.B.C. & A. A.D.S.S./Forms/C. 2118.

WAR DIARY
or
INTELLIGENCE SUMMARY

(Erase heading not required.)

Army Form C. 2118

Place	Date	Hour	Summary of Events and Information	Remarks and references to Appendices
ACHEUX	14/9/16	10 a.m.	Inspected billets & sanitation of Brit. Inf. Divnl. Reserve Coy., billets clean but yards want cleaning up, and manure want removing.	
"	"	11 a.m.	Visited billets of 36th Divnl. Reserve Coy., these billets not kept in accordance with Divnl. Orders, instructed D.m. Commandant to see these done.	
"	"	12 p.m.	Inspected billets & sanitation of O.D. Battery 153 Brigade R.G.A. found billets very dirty, closed yards, reported matter to H.Q. R.A.	
"	"	2 p.m.	Inspected billets of 16½ Royal Irish Rifles, satisfactory.	
"	"	3 p.m.	Inspected billets and saw sanitary arrangements of 194th Heavy Battery R.G.A. very excellent	

Army Form C. 2118

WAR DIARY
or
INTELLIGENCE SUMMARY
(Erase heading not required.)

Instructions regarding War Diaries and Intelligence Summaries are contained in F.S. Regs., Part II. and the Staff Manual respectively. Title Pages will be prepared in manuscript.

Place	Date	Hour	Summary of Events and Information	Remarks and references to Appendices
MARTIN-SART.	15/3/16	11 a.m.	Inspected billets & sanitary arrangements of 14th Reserve Park A.S.C. Very dirty; reported to H.Q.	
"	"	12 p.m.	Ditto. 9th Royal Inniskilling Fusiliers. Found in transport section of the regiment, men three lying together in same billets, saw Regimental Commandant and O/c transport and ordered all horses to be removed from the billets. Reported to H.Q.	
"	"	2 p.m.	Inspected billets & sanitary arrangements of 10th Royal Inniskilling Fusiliers. Found billets, yards & surroundances all dirty; reported to H.Q.	
"	"	3 p.m.	Inspected billets & sanitary arrangements of 121 Coy R.E. Very satisfactory. Reported verbally to A.D.M.S. 36th Div. of MARTINSART re insanitary condition & drew some attention to sanitation by O/C's	

1875 Wt. W593/826 1,000,000 4/15 J.B.C. & A. A.D.S.S./Forms/C. 2118.

WAR DIARY or INTELLIGENCE SUMMARY

Army Form C. 2118

Place	Date	Hour	Summary of Events and Information	Remarks and references to Appendices
BEAU-SSART	16/3/16	10 a.m.	Units mo. discovery fell Battle of the Divps. Inspected billets of 9th Royal Irish Rifles at BEAUSSART. School Tailoring.	
"	"	11 a.m.	Inspected billets of 154 Brigade R.F.A. School Tailoring.	
"	"	12 p.m.	Inspected billets of 46th Heavy Brigade R.G.A. School Tailoring.	
"	"	2 p.m.	Inspected billets of Sanitary arrangements of Ammunition Column very satisfactory.	
"	"	3 p.m.	Inspected billets of Anti-air craft section R.A. School Tailoring.	

Army Form C. 2118

WAR DIARY
or
INTELLIGENCE SUMMARY
(Erase heading not required.)

Place	Date	Hour	Summary of Events and Information	Remarks and references to Appendices
FORCE-VILLE	7/3/16	10 am	Inspected billets of Transport section of 9th, 10th & 11th Royal Irish Rifles. Satisfactory.	
"	"	12 pm	Inspected billets Sanitary arrangements of 4th Piermont R/r. Satisfactory.	
ACHEUX	"	2 pm	Saw new latrine which is in course of construction by my men at the ruinic ACHEUX.	
"	"	4 pm	Inspected new type of urinal (Army 2 types) built by my men at the Aid Posts office.	
"	"	5 pm	Sent in a Sanitary report on the various villages in the Division to the ADMS 36th Division.	

WAR DIARY
or
INTELLIGENCE SUMMARY
(Erase heading not required.)

Army Form C. 2118

Place	Date	Hour	Summary of Events and Information	Remarks and references to Appendices
ACHEUX	18/3/16	12 p.m.	Ordered by ADMS 36th Division to proceed to MARTINSART for sanitation of this town.	
MARTIN SART	19/3/16	10 am	Arrived MARTINSART with Sergeant and 3 men, met Town Commandant and Lt/Qb Captain of 109th Brigade, who led a fatigue party lot of N/6. Had large open frame in middle of town cleared up of old bottles, tins, dustcarts, decomposing food etc.	
"	"	3 p.m.	Had open frame at South end of town cleared up.	
"	20/3/16	9 a.m.	Had yard in which mules are stabled cleaned up, front soakpit dug for kitchens, kitchens cleared out, manure removed, and foul drains dug, also drain dug from kitchen at Chateau to soak, and an old soakpit to filled in & put one inside.	

Army Form C. 2118

WAR DIARY
or
INTELLIGENCE SUMMARY
(Erase heading not required.)

Instructions regarding War Diaries and Intelligence Summaries are contained in F. S. Regs., Part II. and the Staff Manual respectively. Title Pages will be prepared in manuscript.

Place	Date	Hour	Summary of Events and Information	Remarks and references to Appendices
MARTIN-SART	20/9/16	6 a.m.	Had billets at various parts of town cleared out, all the old bits of wood & wire removed throut, arranged with Royal Engineers to break all billets.	
"	21/9/16	9 a.m.	Cleared up more billets. Royal Engineers started breaking billets.	
"	22/9/16	9 a.m.	5th having billets cleaned up. Had Pond, which was in a very insanitary state, at lower end of town drained.	
"	23/9/16	9 a.m.	Had several yards of billets cleaned up & small cess pools also filled in.	
"	24/9/16	9 a.m.	ditto.	
"	25/9/16	9 a.m.	ditto. Had insanitary pond in centre of town cleaned	

WAR DIARY
or
INTELLIGENCE SUMMARY
(Erase heading not required.)

Army Form C. 2118

Place	Date	Hour	Summary of Events and Information	Remarks and references to Appendices
MARTIN-SART	26/3/16	9 a.m.	orders been received that all horses will be taken out to Stables & Stables tanked for men, had a number of Stables cleaned out, refer to Jurnlt.	
"	27/3/16	9 a.m.	Ditto. When three of Stables were deposited had also filled in with chalk & bricks & the disinfected after cleaning.	
"	28/3/16	9 a.m.	Went round various billets, which 2nd Lieut been tasked with Brig admin 109th Brigade, had done Stables cleaned out.	
"	29/3/16	9 a.m.	Received notes to which to H.Q. went round all billets & saw all Sanitary arrangements with Town Commandant and Staff Captain.	
HAPTON-VILLE	30/3/16	9 a.m.	Received notes to proceed to HAPTONVILLE. arrived & proceeded with my fatigue party to clean up the infants-billets & yards in the Town.	
"	31/3/16	9 a.m.	Ditto.	

76 Sanitee Vol 5

Confidential

War Diary of Capt G. Davies R.A.M.C
O.C. 76th Sanitary Section.
36th Division.

To
The Officer,
i/c Adjutant Generals Office, at the Base

April 9/16

WAR DIARY
or
INTELLIGENCE SUMMARY
(Erase heading not required.)

Army Form C. 2118

Place	Date	Hour	Summary of Events and Information	Remarks and references to Appendices
HARPONVILLE	1/4/16	9/30 a.m	Had a number of latrines & the Dixon cleared out, urine pits made behind each hut + trench latrines dug pro tem. Tested the water in all five wells in the village, found 3 used latrine was built of wood & felt for the Turkish system	
"	2/4/16	9/30 a.m	Drills. A latrine was built of wood & felt for the Turkish system for the convenience of 200 men, also a urine pit made with a trough to prevent fouling the ground.	
"	3/4/16	10 a.m	Arrived with my unit from ACHEUX, started to build Field Kitchen + Ovens. Inspected billets for Divisional Troops who arrived today.	
"	4/4/16	9 a.m	Ordered Carried incinerator to be built for burning forecast matter? at my billets, also an incinerator at H.Q. Kitchen.	

Army Form C. 2118

WAR DIARY
or
INTELLIGENCE SUMMARY
(Erase heading not required.)

Place	Date	Hour	Summary of Events and Information	Remarks and references to Appendices
HARPONVILLE	5/4/16	6 a.m.	Had officers of ADMS 36th Division dressed out again. Arranged for latrines being built at officers' also huts - latrines, and urinals for No. 45 billets. Had a ride also built at HQ offrs. Q head.	
LEAL-VILLERS	"	p.m.	Inspected some after SlothB which we hand to hibits for men, but then cleared out & disinfected.	
HARPONVILLE	6/4/16	9 a.m.	Had an incredible built for HQ Officers Q head. Inspected new kitchen built for the Q Corps. Arranged with Town Commandant to have new hotels to be put in each well, + that all manure be removed by civilians.	

WAR DIARY
or
INTELLIGENCE SUMMARY
(Erase heading not required.)

Army Form C. 2118

Instructions regarding War Diaries and Intelligence Summaries are contained in F.S. Regs., Part II. and the Staff Manual respectively. Title Pages will be prepared in manuscript.

Place	Date	Hour	Summary of Events and Information	Remarks and references to Appendices
HARPON- VILLE	7/4/16	9.30 a.m.	Inspected all billets in HARPONVILLE and saw that sanitary arrangements were correct.	
MARTIN- SART	8/4/16	10 a.m.	Went to MARTINSART with the DADMS 36th Division, inspected billets & sanitary arrangements there. Found the many white billets try ants were far from clean; reported to ADMS 36th Division, saw new drain built from baths to top pond and advised that a proper soak pit should be dug.	
TOUTEN- COURT.	9/4/16	9.30 a.m.	Inspected 172 Brigade R.F.A., found all unit and saw their new Army Unit attached to 10 Btalps, a them in Julian.	
LEAL- VILLERS	12/4/16	9.30 a.m.	Rode over to LEALVILLERS & saw the Town Commandant arranged with him to have 6 number of Stables disinfected which I consider he looked for close billeting.	

Army Form C. 2118

WAR DIARY
or
INTELLIGENCE SUMMARY
(Erase heading not required.)

Place	Date	Hour	Summary of Events and Information	Remarks and references to Appendices
HARPON-VILLE	11/4/16	9-30 a.m.	Had a new type of urinal built, a pit 10-4 feet deep now is dug & filled in with stones, a pipe leads from the centre of the stones empty petrol tins about 4 ft within of pit through the stones. This makes a much cleaner urinal & prevents pooling of ground.	
PUCH-VILLERS	12/4/16	10 a.m.	Saw Dnn Commandant of PUCHVILLERS and inspected all billets and sanitary arrangements with I men, found everything in a very satisfactory condition.	
VARENNES	13/4/16	10 a.m.	Saw Dnn Commandant of VARENNES and inspected all billets & sanitary arrangements. Satisfactory.	
FORCE-VILLE	14/4/16	10 a.m.	Inspected SWW Artillery & Royal Engineers billets & sanitary arrangements. Satisfactory. Saw Dnn Commandant and arranged with him and burying arrangements of men in FORCEVILLE	

WAR DIARY
or
INTELLIGENCE SUMMARY
(Erase heading not required.)

Army Form C. 2118

Place	Date	Hour	Summary of Events and Information	Remarks and references to Appendices
HARPON-VILLE	15/4/16	10/30 a.m.	Accompanied the ADMS 36th Division around some of the Billets in HARPONVILLE, & also inspected the Sanitary arrangements and informed us he was satisfied with everything we saw	
"	16/4/16	9/30 a.m.	Inspected the huts, billets & sanitary arrangements of the Brigade ammunition Column of the 153rd Brigade R.F.A., also the 36th Divisional Signal Coy & found all correct.	
HENDAU-VILLE	17/4/16	9/30 a.m.	Went to HEADAUVILLE to inspect the sanitary arrangements of this Town. It is proposed to move Divisional HQrs. here on the 20th inst. Found a good deal of sanitary work required doing, arranged with the Town Major to bring more men of my Unit over tomorrow 15/4/16	

WAR DIARY
or
INTELLIGENCE SUMMARY
(Erase heading not required.)

Army Form C. 2118

Place	Date	Hour	Summary of Events and Information	Remarks and references to Appendices
HEDAU-VILLE	18/4/16	10 a.m.	Arrived with 4 cars from Army Hdqts & proceeded to close onto the Chateau at HEDAUVILLE for H.Q., 9 other huts are in course of being set up between in the grounds for use of H.Q. units.	
"	19/4/16	10 a.m.	Started to turn the pond in the Chateau yard, had all rubbish in this pond, cleared out & disinfected, also the entrances & exits all wells & had them cleaned out & disinfected.	
"	20/4/16	10 a.m.	Arrived at HEDAUVILLE with my Unit, had an Armstrong Hut erected as my Billet & Office, had an interior for it up for H.Q. at Chateau and also behind H.Q. Offices.	
"	21/4/16	10 a.m.	Tested the water of the few wells of the town and found the water in each well required 1 grain of bleaching powder to chlorinate the amount of water contained in one dinner water flask.	

Army Form C. 2118

WAR DIARY
or
INTELLIGENCE SUMMARY
(Erase heading not required.)

Instructions regarding War Diaries and Intelligence Summaries are contained in F.S. Regs., Part II. and the Staff Manual respectively. Title Pages will be prepared in manuscript.

Place	Date	Hour	Summary of Events and Information	Remarks and references to Appendices
TOUTEN- COURT	22/4/16	11 am	Went to TOUTENCOURT to inspect 3 coys of my Unit employed at Corps HQ and to enquire how Sergeant was being carried out. Found it was satisfactory.	
PUCHE-VILLERS	"	3 pm	Went to PUCHEVILLERS & inspected Sanitary arrangements Hutts-36th Division Ammunition Column who are under canvas. Also inspected the Supply Column. Satisfactory.	
HEDAU-VILLE	23/4/16	9/30 am	Saw Lieutenant Col. g.a. Royal Irish Rifles about a sanitary point at his laundry which is insanitary; arranged with his Divn. Sanitary Officer to get on track.	
"	"	11 am	Had arrival & breakfast for hatrun work Sanitary Officers huts, and arranged to have bins in which trash for HQ Officers.	

Army Form C. 2118

WAR DIARY
or
INTELLIGENCE SUMMARY
(Erase heading not required.)

Instructions regarding War Diaries and Intelligence Summaries are contained in F.S. Regs., Part II. and the Staff Manual respectively. Title Pages will be prepared in manuscript.

Place	Date	Hour	Summary of Events and Information	Remarks and references to Appendices
HEDAUVILLE	24/4/16		Holiday granted to Division by Divisional Commander.	
MARTINSART	25/4/16	10/30 a.m.	Visited MARTINSART & Read to Willows of the 14th R.I.Rif. sprayed in which seven to seven meals had occurred. Inspected the billets & sanitary arrangements of the HQ 109th Brigade. HQ 108th Brigade and 122, 150 & 121 Coys Royal Engineers, all satisfactory.	
FORCEVILLE	26/4/16	11 a.m.	Visited FORCEVILLE and saw billets & sanitary arrangements of 154th Brigade R.F.A. - satisfactory.	
VARENNES	"	3 p.m.	Visited VARENNES & saw the sanitary arrangements of the 109th Field Ambulance, satisfactory.	

Army Form C. 2118

WAR DIARY
or
INTELLIGENCE SUMMARY
(Erase heading not required.)

Instructions regarding War Diaries and Intelligence Summaries are contained in F.S. Regs, Part II. and the Staff Manual respectively. Title Pages will be prepared in manuscript.

Place	Date	Hour	Summary of Events and Information	Remarks and references to Appendices
HEDAUVILLE	27/4/16	9:30 a.m.	Arranged to empty pond which is very insanitary at the Chateau HEDAUVILLE but found the Royal Engineers had sent pumping plant.	
"	"	10-30 a.m.	Inspected all the Royal Artillery lines and found everything satisfactory.	
PUCHE-VILLERS	"	3 p.m.	Inspected the billets & saw the sanitary arrangements of the 36th Division Cavalry at Puchevillers and found everything satisfactory.	
HAR-PONVILLE	"	5:30 p.m.	Inspected the billets & saw the sanitary arrangements of the Mobile Veterinary Section at HARPONVILLE. Satisfactory.	
HEDAU-VILLE	28/4/16		Nothing to report	
HEDAU-VILLE	29/4/16	5 a.m.	Proceeded on ten days leave to England.	

1875 Wt. W593/826 1,000,000 4/15 J.B.C. & A. A.D.S.S./Forms/C. 2118.

Confidential.

War Diary of Capt. J. Davies, R.A.M.C.
D.O., 76th Sanitary Sec:
76th Division

76 San Sec
R.A.M.C.

Month 5/16

To...

The Officer,
i/c Adjutant General's Office,
Base.

COMMITTEE FOR THE
MEDICAL HISTORY OF THE WAR
Date 26 JUN 1916

Army Form C. 2118.

WAR DIARY
or
INTELLIGENCE SUMMARY
(Erase heading not required.)

Instructions regarding War Diaries and Intelligence Summaries are contained in F. S. Regs., Part II. and the Staff Manual respectively. Title Pages will be prepared in manuscript.

Place	Date	Hour	Summary of Events and Information	Remarks and references to Appendices
McDonville	1/5/16	7 p.m.	On the departure of the O.C. 76 Sanitary Section (Capt. Davis) on leave, Lieut. W.S.B. Hay took command. According to instructions received from A.D.M.S. 36 Division Parenium was inspected and found to be in satisfactory condition as regards sanitation.	
"	2/5/16	"	The inspection of Hartmille was carried out. The sanitation of that town was found to be satisfactory.	
"	3/5/16	"	The day was spent in inspecting Picquiere. No insanitary conditions were found.	
"	4/5/16	"	A sanitary inspection of McDonville and of the woods near the town occupied by billeting of various units was made.	
"	5/5/16	"	The 8th Batt. R.I. Rifles & 10 batt. R.I. Rifles & 36 Div. Train were inspected and found to be good as regards sanitation.	
"	6/5/16	"	The Bruchvilliers was found expected and found with the sanitary measures taken by the 36 Div. Amm. Col. & 36th Div. Cavalry.	
"	7/5/16	"	Nothing to report	
"	8/5/16	"	"	
"	9/5/16	"	Nothing to report	

Army Form C. 2118.

WAR DIARY
or
INTELLIGENCE SUMMARY
(Erase heading not required.)

Instructions regarding War Diaries and Intelligence Summaries are contained in F. S. Regs., Part II. and the Staff Manual respectively. Title Pages will be prepared in manuscript.

Place	Date	Hour	Summary of Events and Information	Remarks and references to Appendices
HEDAUVILLE	10/5/16	7 p.m.	Arrived back from leave and reported arrived to ADMS 36th Division	
"	11/5/16	9/30 a.m.	Inspected the Sanitary arrangements in the town of HEDAUVILLE. Arranged to have a new Horsefall Destructor erected.	
PUCHVILLERS	12/5/16	10/30 a.m.	Went to PUCHVILLERS and inspected the Sanitary arrangements of the Inniskilling Dragoons, Divisional Ammunition Column and Royal Engineers of the 44th Division. Found every thing satisfactory.	
HARPON- VILLE	13/5/16	10 a.m.	Went to HARPONVILLE and inspected the Mobile Veterinary Sections Sanitary arrangements, very satisfactory. Saw Sanitary arrangements of Ammunition Column of 157th & 158th Brigades R.F.A. satisfactory.	

2449 Wt. W14957/M90 750,000 1/16 J.B.C. & A. Forms/C.2118/12.

Army Form C. 2118.

WAR DIARY
or
INTELLIGENCE SUMMARY
(Erase heading not required.)

Instructions regarding War Diaries and Intelligence Summaries are contained in F. S. Regs., Part II. and the Staff Manual respectively. Title Pages will be prepared in manuscript.

Place	Date	Hour	Summary of Events and Information	Remarks and references to Appendices
FORCE-VILLE	14/7/16	10 a.m.	Went to Toutencourt and saw the Sanitary arrangements of the 154th Brigade R.G.A. also of the 9th and 10th Royal Inniskilling Fusiliers. Found billets clean and sanitary arrangements satisfactory.	
VARENNES	15/7/16	10 a.m.	Went to VARENNES and saw the Sanitary arrangements of the Divisional Supply Column, 109th Field Ambulance, Advance Stores and Military Mounted Police. Found every thing satisfactory.	
HEDAU-VILLE	16/7/16	9/30 a.m.	Made a Sanitary inspection of HEDAUVILLE Wood and found the R.G.A. units were being ins anitary. Matters for some of them were ordered. Part this taken down and horses lst billeted in the trees and saw the Sanitary arrangements of the Units in the Chateau grounds, found them satisfactory.	

2449 Wt. W14957/Mgo 750,000 1/16 J.B.C. & A. Forms/C.2118/12.

WAR DIARY
or
INTELLIGENCE SUMMARY

Army Form C. 2118

Place	Date	Hour	Summary of Events and Information	Remarks and references to Appendices
FORCE-VILLE	7/5/16	10 am	Inspected at FORCEVILLE Sanitary Arrangements of the 105th Heavy Battery R.G.A., 15th Royal Irish Rifles, and 8th Mahratta Regt. Found the arrangements satisfactory. Joined wells in all four wells at Forceville and found that each well water required an increase of Bleaching Powder to disinfect it per service indent.	
LEAL-VILLERS	8/5/16	10 am	Inspected Sanitary arrangements at LEALVILLERS of the Divisional Train, the 10th and 11th Royal Irish Rifles. Found everything satisfactory. Tested Wells in well No 3 in LEALVILLERS which is short. Also taken into use and found it required an increase of Bleaching powder to disinfect the water per service indent.	

WAR DIARY
or
INTELLIGENCE SUMMARY
(Erase heading not required.)

Army Form C. 2118

Place	Date	Hour	Summary of Events and Information	Remarks and references to Appendices
HEDAU-VILLE and	19/5/16	10 am	Inspected the Sanitary arrangements of HEDAUVILLE with the officer Major HEDAUVILLE, ordered several French Latrines to be filled in and the present supply of Latrine bts. used. Started to build a large incinerator at the bottom end of road from the entrance road to HEDAUVILLE	
HARPONVILLE	20/5/16	10 am	Inspected all the wells in HARPONVILLE and again with Ito stretcher beaver, found the resalt [illegible] and will make required imrovements of trenches [illegible] to eliminate it for service materials.	
HEDAU-VILLE	21/5/16	10 am	Inspected new baths being erected by the 173rd Brigade R.E. on the Senlis Road with the O.C. NS 36 Division and found every thing satisfactory	

WAR DIARY
or
INTELLIGENCE SUMMARY
(Erase heading not required.)

Army Form C. 2118

Place	Date	Hour	Summary of Events and Information	Remarks and references to Appendices
HEDAU- VILLE	27/5/16	10 a.m.	Inspected the Sanitary arrangements & saw the Horse Lines of all the Artillery Units in HEDAUVILLE, found everything satisfactory with the exception of Bernard's manure, which is not taken far enough away from the Lines in hery dumpcart instead of being spread. Ordered manure to be taken at least 500 yards away from the lines and the manure to be spread not dumped.	
VARENNES	29/5/16	10 a.m.	Inspected M. Powells in VARENNES and told Powells to sink a few wells. Ordered in cart with requisite conveniences & flushing powder to Utimate it, per service who car. Tested also troughs from the new pipe supply at Varennes. Do not want one from CONTAY and does not require any attention	

WAR DIARY
or
INTELLIGENCE SUMMARY
(Erase heading not required.)

Army Form C. 2118

Instructions regarding War Diaries and Intelligence Summaries are contained in F.S. Regs., Part II. and the Staff Manual respectively. Title Pages will be prepared in manuscript.

Place	Date	Hour	Summary of Events and Information	Remarks and references to Appendices
FORCE-VILLE	24/5/16	10/a.m	Inspected the Sanitary arrangements of all the Units in FORCE-VILLE and found everything satisfactory except too much manure is allowed to accumulate in rear of Billyards. Ordered the Town Major to have the manure removed by the troops.	
HARPON-VILLE	25/5/16	10 a.m	Inspected the Sanitary Arrangements of all Units in HARPONVILLE and found every Bty satisfactory. Instructed the Town Major to have all manure removed from yard of billets stored and not dumped as is being done at present.	
VAREN-NES	26/5/16	10 a.m	Inspected the Sanitary arrangements of the Divisional Supply Column and Nº 70 q 1st Field Ambulance at VARENNES & found everything very satisfactory	

WAR DIARY
or
INTELLIGENCE SUMMARY

Army Form C. 2118.

Place	Date	Hour	Summary of Events and Information	Remarks and references to Appendices
LEAL-VILLERS	27/5/16	10 a.m.	Inspected the Sanitary arrangements of new billets of Mt. Divisional Supply Column and found them satisfactory. Arranged with Return Major to have a final chemical [?] reexamination.	
HEDAU-VILLE	28/5/16	10 a.m.	Inspected the sanitary arrangements of Head Quarter Units and found every thing satisfactory. Arranged with the Town Major to have a cess pool filled in near the entrance to the town.	
AEDAU-VILLE	29/5/16	10 a.m.	92 Germans have shelled the new Railhead at ACHEUX during danger running. I went on to FORCEVILLE to see if any damage had been done to the pipe make supply and found the pipe had been broken by a shell near the pumping station and the supply cut off.	

WAR DIARY
or
INTELLIGENCE SUMMARY

(Erase heading not required.)

Army Form C. 2118.

Place	Date	Hour	Summary of Events and Information	Remarks and references to Appendices
HEDAU-VILLE	29/5/16	4 p.m.	Attended a conference of all Divn Rep^ns and the C.A.T.O.R.E. of 32nd Division on the removal and disposal of manure. It was arranged that an all manure arrived from pits to at least 500 yards from villages to prevent with local self dumpers.	
FORCE-VILLE	30/5/16	10 a.m.	Inspected Sanitary arrangements of all units in FORCEVILLE and found everything satisfactory. Germans are still shelling Hersailleul at ACHEUX and BUS for supply of water to FORCEVILLE is still cut off.	
VARENNES	31/5/16	10 a.m.	Inspected the sanitary arrangements of the West Riding Artillery rendered proper Latrines & urine pits to be made. Saw Divn Maj^r on dispord of manure in VARENNES	
HARPON-VILLE	1/6/16	12/30 p.m.	Saw Divn Repr on dispord of manure in HARPONVILLE. Inspected H.Q units of 105th Brigade and ordered pro^r urine pits & Soak pits to be built.	

76 San. Sec.
Vol 7
Germ

"Scout"
Jun 1916

War Diary

O.C. 76th Sanitary

COMMITTEE FOR THE
MEDICAL HISTORY OF THE WAR
5 AUG 1915
Date

June 30th 1916

WAR DIARY
or
INTELLIGENCE SUMMARY

(Erase heading not required.)

Army Form C. 2118.

Place	Date	Hour	Summary of Events and Information	Remarks and references to Appendices
HEDAU-VILLE	1/6/16	9/30	Inspected the Sanitation of the town of HEDAUVILLE and found it satisfactory, ordered all manure which is removed from yards & billets/stables to be spread on the land and not dumped. A covered incinerator is being built behind billet No 4, 3 to burn excreta & so top the end of the village	
FORCE-VILLE	2/6/16	9/30	Inspected all the R.A. horse lines in FORCEVILLE, ordered all manure which is taken from these lines to be spread in the land. and a new line pit to be built in the horse lines of 172nd Brigade R.F.A.	
VAREN-NES	3/6/16	9/30	Inspected the billets & saw sanitary arrangements of D.A.C. at VARENNES, ordered pupees incinerator to be built.	

Army Form C. 2118

WAR DIARY
or
INTELLIGENCE SUMMARY
(Erase heading not required.)

Instructions regarding War Diaries and Intelligence Summaries are contained in F. S. Regs., Part II. and the Staff Manual respectively. Title Pages will be prepared in manuscript.

Place	Date	Hour	Summary of Events and Information	Remarks and references to Appendices
HARPON-VILLE	4/6/16	10 a.m.	Inspected Decontamination of the town of HARPONVILLE, also while so doing, ordered new pits for refuse & a new urinal to be made at H Q 10th ? Brigade.	
LEAL-VILLIERS	5/6/16	10 a.m.	Inspected the billets & sanitary arrangements of 1st Divisional train at LEAVILLIERS & found everything in a most satisfactory condition.	
ENGLE-BELMER	6/6/16	11 a.m.	A report has been received that there was an extraordinary Victory of Germans near Englebelmer Wood. I rode out & found a large piece of decomposing meat in a field near the wood. It will be buried with a number of old socks etc. The new incinerator for burning feces etc is now built in HEDAU-VILLE. All excreta is now burnt in this town.	

1875 Wt. W593/826 1,000,000 4/15 J.B.C. & A. A.D.S.S./Forms/C. 2118.

Army Form C. 2118

WAR DIARY
or
INTELLIGENCE SUMMARY

(Erase heading not required.)

Instructions regarding War Diaries and Intelligence Summaries are contained in F. S. Regs., Part II. and the Staff Manual respectively. Title Pages will be prepared in manuscript.

Place	Date	Hour	Summary of Events and Information	Remarks and references to Appendices
HEDAU- VILLE WOOD.	7/6/16	9/30	Inspected all the lines have & sanitary arrangements of the R.a. in HEDAUVILLE WOOD. Found everything satisfactory. All manure is now being disposed of by burial.	
VAREN- NES	8/6/16	10 a.m.	Went on to VARENNES to see Lt Dunn again with regard to drawing a large cess-pit in a yard occupied by the A.O.D. Arranged with him to get a pump and a hand liquid manure cart to Dunn it emptied and spread over the yard. The farmer who owns the yard.	
CLAIR- FAYE	9/6/16	11 a.m.	Inspected the billets & saw the sanitary arrangements of the 109th and 110th Field Ambulances, found everything perfectly satisfactory	

Army Form C. 2118.

WAR DIARY
or
INTELLIGENCE SUMMARY

(Erase heading not required.)

Instructions regarding War Diaries and Intelligence Summaries are contained in F. S. Regs., Part II. and the Staff Manual respectively. Title Pages will be prepared in manuscript.

Place	Date	Hour	Summary of Events and Information	Remarks and references to Appendices
LEAL-VILLERS	10/9/16	10 a.m.	Inspected the Sanitation, water supply etc of the lines of LEALVILLERS with the Sann Major. Found everything satisfactory.	
YHREN-NES	11/9/16	9 a.m.	Inspected the billets & New Sanitation arrangements of the 11th Royal Irish Rifles, Inniskillings, Div. Supply Column, Div. Amm Column, Army Veterinary Stores, 247th Brigade R.F.A. & 6th Dorks Rehm Regiments, ordered new latrines to be built by the D.A.C. & 247th Brigade R.F.A. the 11th Royal Inniskilling Fusiliers & Div Supply Column were very satisfactory. & formed D.A.D.V.S. that the latrines were Really be put Around.	
FORCE-VILLE	12/9/16	10 a.m.	Inspected the billets & water & sanitation arrangements of Batterries Units in FORCEVILLE with the D.a.D.n.S 36th Division & found everything very satisfactory.	

2449 Wt. W14957/M90 750,000 1/16 J.B.C. & A. Forms/C.2118/12.

WAR DIARY
or
INTELLIGENCE SUMMARY
(Erase heading not required.)

Army Form C. 2118.

Place	Date	Hour	Summary of Events and Information	Remarks and references to Appendices
VAREN- NES.	13/9/16	10 a.m.	Inspected the Baths which are being made at VARENNES and arranged for a grease trap to be made there. Talk moved to make seats for water lorry to be used as ambulance for sitting down cases in order than any water lorry as an ambulance for sitting down cases should an emergency arise. A Water lorry has now been parked in No 3 Public Hedauville for use in the Division & a number of blankets despatched.	
HEDAU- VILLE Wood	14/9/16	10 a.m.	Inspected the Sanitary arrangements of the various Units in HEDAUVILLE Wood. These were satisfactory.	
HARPON- VILLE	15/9/16	a.m.	Inspected the Sanitary arrangements of the various Units in HARPONVILLE. These were found satisfactory.	

Army Form C. 2118.

WAR DIARY
or
INTELLIGENCE SUMMARY
(Erase heading not required.)

Instructions regarding War Diaries and Intelligence Summaries are contained in F. S. Regs., Part II. and the Staff Manual respectively. Title Pages will be prepared in manuscript.

Place	Date	Hour	Summary of Events and Information	Remarks and references to Appendices
WAREN-MES.	16/9/16	10 a.m.	Inspected the sanitary arrangements of the Divisional Supply Column and 246th Brigade R.F.A. Found them satisfactory.	
FORCE-VILLE	17/9/16	9/30 a.m.	Inspected with the Town Major the Billets & sanitary arrangements of the new Units arrived in FORCEVILLE, found them satisfactory.	
HEDAU-VILLERS	18/9/16	10 a.m.	Inspected the Huts & sanitary arrangements of the 1/5 KOYLI & the Malt Drill Horse, ordered the lines of the Pickets to be kept cleaner and the manure from the lines to be removed & spread out dumped in the road.	
LEAL-VILIERS	19/9/16	10 a.m.	Inspected the Billets & saw the Sanitary arrangements of the Divisional Train. Found everything most satisfactory.	

2449 Wt. W14957/Mg0 750,000 1/16 J.B.C. & A. Forms/C.2118/12.

WAR DIARY or INTELLIGENCE SUMMARY

Army Form C. 2118

Place	Date	Hour	Summary of Events and Information	Remarks and references to Appendices
HEDAU-VILLE	20/9/16	9/30 a.m.	Visited H.Q.'s respectively the H.Q. Units 36th Division and of the R.A. Units. The billets were very dirty & unhealthy. The Sanitary arrangements were satisfactory. Reported the Units to C.R.A.	
VAREN-NES	21/9/16	10 a.m.	Arranged with the Town Major VARENNES, leaving for the Battle the 2nd in Command, going under to take the 1/5 & 1/0 4 2 I (better than Commun). Ordered the Jordan Lorry to the 110th Field Ambulance at CLAIRFAYE for disinfecting clothing.	
CLAIR-FAYE	22/9/16	10 a.m.	Inspected the Sanitary arrangement of the 109th and 110th Field Ambulance. Found everything very satisfactory.	

Army Form C. 2118

WAR DIARY
or
INTELLIGENCE SUMMARY
(Erase heading not required.)

Instructions regarding War Diaries and Intelligence Summaries are contained in F. S. Regs., Part II. and the Staff Manual respectively. Title Pages will be prepared in manuscript.

Place	Date	Hour	Summary of Events and Information	Remarks and references to Appendices
HEDAU-VILLE	23/6/16	9/00 a.m.	Three batteries of French Artillery Army arrived in HEDAUVILLE. Have ordered my Vets to assist veterans examine picks for their Divisional class are being built by the French troops. Inspected them, billets & water servers, arrangements for sick pile to be made near these quarters.	
HARPON-VILLE	24/6/16	10 a.m.	Visited with the Div. Major at HARPONVILLE the billets and saw the Sanitary arrangements of the 4th M.T. British train and 36th D.A.C. Found everything satisfactory.	
FORCE-VILLE	25/6/16	10 a.m.	Visited with the Div. Major at FORCEVILLE, billets and saw the Sanitary arrangements of the two units arrived in FORCEVILLE. Have now found John Godwin.	

WAR DIARY
or
INTELLIGENCE SUMMARY
(Erase heading not required.)

Army Form C. 2118

Place	Date	Hour	Summary of Events and Information	Remarks and references to Appendices
LEAL-VILLERS	26/6/16	10 a.m.	Inspected the billets & sanitary arrangements of the Units in LEAL-VILLERS, also the water supply. Found everything satisfactory.	
HEDAU-VILLE	27/6/16	9.30 a.m.	Inspected the Huts in October grounds occupied by the Cheshire Section R.E. Ordered some alterations the trestle & feet. Water supply satisfactory.	
VARENNES	28/6/16	10 a.m.	Inspected the Baths at VARENNES with the Inn. Major of same Bat. Satisfactory arrangements by the Divisional Supply Column.	
HEDAU-VILLE	29/6/16	6/30 a.m.	Nothing to report	
HEDAU-VILLE	30/6/16	6/30 a.m.	Nothing to report	

Secret

36 Army
76. San Sec
Vol 8

War Diary
of
O.C. 76th Sanitary Section

July 1916.

COMMITTEE FOR ...
MEDICAL HISTORY OF THE WAR
Date 5 - SEP 1916

WAR DIARY
or
INTELLIGENCE SUMMARY
(Erase heading not required.)

Army Form C. 2118.

Place	Date	Hour	Summary of Events and Information	Remarks and references to Appendices
HEDAU-VILLE	July 1st	6 am	The 36th Division attacked. I was ordered by the ADMS 36th Division to report to duty, my men were sent to act as Bearer Carriers, we have some Enfield Rifleman, we sent as Medical orderly with the Sanitary M.Mr. Lorry which was used as an Ambulance.	
"	"	10 am	Sent by the ADMS to Transport Station on the ENCELBELMER BOUZANCOURT Road where a number of men were attended with shell shock by the M.O'/c. Dr Smith & myself. I went then & examined two hundred & fifty-two cases, sending most of them back with hitcha after a rest.	
"	July 2nd	10 am	Proceeded again to the Dumfort Station, very few cases took afforded and those that lost afforded were sent back with Ambulance after a rest.	
"	"	11 am	Proceeded to MARTINSART and saw the DaDMS 86th Division and adjusted within that few cases of Shell Shock had been dealt with	

Army Form C. 2118.

WAR DIARY
or
INTELLIGENCE SUMMARY
(Erase heading not required.)

Instructions regarding War Diaries and Intelligence Summaries are contained in F. S. Regs., Part II. and the Staff Manual respectively. Title Pages will be prepared in manuscript.

Place	Date	Hour	Summary of Events and Information	Remarks and references to Appendices
HEDAU-VILLE	July 2/16	10 p.m.	Driving at Mr Rowefout Station.	
"	July 3/16	10 a.m.	Reported to the CDMS 36th Division for duty.	
"	July 4/16	10 a.m.	Proceeded to MARTINSART with a fuel of Ambulances to collect Wounded from the Schyzen front on the MESNIL Road, returned to HEDAUVILLE with the DADMS 36th Division.	
"	July 5/16	10 a.m.	Inspected with the Area Major all billets in HEDAUVILLE and ordered some billets to be cleaned up which had been left in an insanitary condition.	
"	"	"	Ordered to RUBEMPRE on the 6th, cleaned up the trenches of the 76th Division Cavalry and worked up army stores.	
"	July 6/16	9 a.m.	Proceeded to RUBEMPRE and took over billets for Army Units.	

2449 Wt. W14957/M90 750,000 1/16 J.B.C. & A. Forms/C.2118/12.

WAR DIARY or INTELLIGENCE SUMMARY

Army Form C. 2118.

(Erase heading not required.)

Instructions regarding War Diaries and Intelligence Summaries are contained in F. S. Regs., Part II. and the Staff Manual respectively. Title Pages will be prepared in manuscript.

Place	Date	Hour	Summary of Events and Information	Remarks and references to Appendices
RUBEM-PRE	July 8/16	9 a.m.	Proceeded to mill, inspected field kitchen and put up pumps. Latrines & dry urine pit for use of my Unit.	
"	July 8/16	9 a.m.	Inspected billets and saw the sanitary arrangements of Head Quarter Units, about incinerator, kitchen, latrines & to be built.	
"	July 9/16	6 a.m.	Orders having been received to march to BERNAVILLE on the 10th July 1916 I had the camps of my Unit cleaned up and my straw packed.	
BERNA-VILLE	July 10/16	6 a.m.	Proceeded with my Unit to BERNAVILLE and took over billets. Got latrines control and a field kitchen built.	
"	July 11/16	9 a.m.	Ordered to proceed to BLERINGHAM. Got my Unit billets cleaned up and my straw packed.	
BLERING-HAM	July 12/16	6 a.m.	Proceeded with my Unit to BLERINGHAM and took over billets for my Unit, erected latrines & built field kitchen.	

Army Form C. 2118.

WAR DIARY
or
INTELLIGENCE SUMMARY
(Erase heading not required.)

Place	Date	Hour	Summary of Events and Information	Remarks and references to Appendices
FILQUES	July 13/16	9 a.m.	Having had return forward to TILQUES, I went there and took over billets for my Units, erected latrines and built field kitchen, also a fatigue party under my own 2nd the Steward who was to the work to H.Q Office cleaned up.	
"	July 14/16	9 a.m.	Had sanitary toilet at my Units billets, saw the sanitary arrangements of H Q units and Mob Veterinary Section, We were satisfactory.	
SETQUES	July 15/16	9 a.m.	Re. D.A.D.M.S 36th Division visited my billets and found them and my sanitary condition satisfactory; proceeded with the D.A.D.M.S 36th Division to SETQUES and inspected the billets and saw the Sanitary arrangements of the 11th Royal Innskillin Fusiliers and found them very satisfactory.	
WATTEN	July 16/16	10 a.m.	Visited WATTEN and saw the billets and sanitary arrangements of the 36th Divisional Train which were very satisfactory.	

WAR DIARY
or
INTELLIGENCE SUMMARY
(Erase heading not required.)

Army Form C. 2118.

Place	Date	Hour	Summary of Events and Information	Remarks and references to Appendices
GANS-PETTE	July 10/16	10 a.m.	Visited GANSPETTE and saw the billets of the 12th Royal Irish Rifles. The sanitary condition of the regiment was very poor, & upon its leaving, grease pits and urine pits are ordered to be emptied.	
MOULLE	July 10/16	10 a.m.	The D.A.D.M.S. Samitation 2nd Army inspected billets & saw the sanitary arrangements of the 16th Royal Irish Rifles & H.M.D.U.L.E. which were found to be satisfactory.	
HOULLE	"	11 a.m.	Proceeded with Sanitary Officer 2nd Army to HOULLE and saw billets & sanitary arrangements of the 12th Royal Irish Rifles which were satisfactory.	
SALPER-WICK	"	1 p.m.	Proceeded with Sanitary Officer 2nd Army to SALPERWICK and saw the Sanitary arrangements of H.Q.'s & No.1 Army Divisional train which were satisfactory.	
"	"	2 p.m.	Saw Sanitary arrangements at Divisional Artillery School of Instruction with Sanitary Officer 2nd Army. A new incinerator was ordered to be built. Also a/c upon milk safe for men, pickles, also fly proof latrines to be made. A large accumulation of manure was ordered to be removed.	

Army Form C. 2118.

WAR DIARY
or
INTELLIGENCE SUMMARY

(Erase heading not required.)

Instructions regarding War Diaries and Intelligence Summaries are contained in F. S. Regs., Part II. and the Staff Manual respectively. Title Pages will be prepared in manuscript.

Place	Date	Hour	Summary of Events and Information	Remarks and references to Appendices
EPER-LECQUES	July 20/16	10 am	Visited 1st & 1st Royal Inniskilling Fusiliers at EPERLECQUES and saw the Sanitary Arrangements which were satisfactory	
TOURNE HEM	"	12 pm	Visited 1st D.A.C. 36th Division at TOURNEHEM and saw the Sanitary Arrangements, a new Unit to me who wished to be briefed.	
ESQUEL-BECK	July 21/16	12 pm	Ordered & proceeded to ESQUELBECK. I looked my night lorry with Stores and proceeded with my Unit and both were billeted, everything in order and had a kitchen.	
"	July 22/16	9 am	Inspected H.Q. Billets which were both fairly listed under supply for troops, ordered all made to be put in a clean state, this was required two menings of cleaning powder for 100 gallons to sterilize it.	
"	"	8 pm	Ordered to proceed to MONTNOIR, I proceeded with my Unit and both were billeted.	

WAR DIARY
or
INTELLIGENCE SUMMARY

Army Form C. 2118.

Place	Date	Hour	Summary of Events and Information	Remarks and references to Appendices
MONT-NOIR	July 23/16	9 a.m.	With a fatigue party under my own Cleared up the Chateau and grounds used as Offices by 36th Divisional Head Quarters. Inspected the water supply, which had broken down and arranged with the Camp Commandant to have Engineers sent to have it repaired. This was done.	
"	"	2 p.m.	Had incinerator and pistol kitchen built on my own bills and scheme created.	
"	July 24/16	9 a.m.	Inside Supply at H.Q.'s again broke down, arranged for Engineers with Camp Commandant to thoroughly overhaul it, had new pit cleared out new Chateau's wire pits dug near latrines and grease pits, master new kitchens.	
"	"	2 p.m.	Inspected water supply on NEUVE EGLISE road, ordered twenty of my men for duty there and arranged with Capt. Hey R.A.M.C. to have bi-hourly samples of water from wells then listed daily for the amount of bleaching powder required to sterilize the water.	

WAR DIARY
or
INTELLIGENCE SUMMARY

(Erase heading not required.)

Army Form C. 2118.

Place	Date	Hour	Summary of Events and Information	Remarks and references to Appendices
BAIL- LEUL	July 25/16	10 a.m.	Went to M Corps HQs and saw the Irish bath officer into report to the bath staffs of the 36th Divisional area.	
"	"	11 a.m.	Visited water supply at NEUVE EGLISE Road and heard the order of plan which I made approved. 1 Division of Yorkshire provided to leave by ?.	
STEEN- WERCHE	"	2 p.m.	Inspected billets and saw the sanitary arrangements of the 121 in by R.E. at STEENWERCHE, ordered for good latrine pits erected.	
MONT- NOIR.	July 26/16	9 a.m.	Ordered my Unit to build models of sanitary appliances to be erected in BAILLEUL	
BAILLEUL	"	11 a.m.	Took over Sanitary duties in billets from 33rd Sanitary Section at BAILLEUL and left him in my car in charge.	
WEST- HOF Farm	"	2 p.m.	Visited A.P.M's mens billets and saw the sanitary arrangements at WESTHOF Farm. Ordered for proper latrines, kitchen and sinks to available covered in trenches	

Army Form C. 2118.

WAR DIARY
or
INTELLIGENCE SUMMARY
(Erase heading not required.)

Instructions regarding War Diaries and Intelligence Summaries are contained in F. S. Regs., Part II. and the Staff Manual respectively. Title Pages will be prepared in manuscript.

Place	Date	Hour	Summary of Events and Information	Remarks and references to Appendices
KORTE PYP Camp	July 27/16	10 a.m.	Visited KORTE PYP Camp which was in a very insanitary condition and arranged with the M.O's of the 8th and 10th Royal Irish Rifles to have the Camp cleaned up, proper latrines, urinals & urine pits made.	
Red Lodge	"	12 p.m.	Visited the Camp at Red Lodge and arranged with the M O's of 1st/4th R.I. Rifles and 11th Inniskilling Fusiliers to have the Camp cleaned up and proper sanitary appliances erected.	
BAILLEUL	July 28/16	10 a.m.	Paid visit to the Ordnance Dumps and arranged with the Ordnance Officer 36th Division to have proper sanitary appliances erected.	
"	"	12 p.m.	Visited the 36th Divisional Train and saw their sanitary arrangements which were very satisfactory, arranged however for few latrines needed.	
BAILLEUL	July 29/16	10 a.m.	Arranged a series of sanitary models at Sanitary Section Camp at BAILLEUL, Stood Sanitary Officers BAILLEUL to see them afterwards inspected all the sanitary arrangements in the town with the Sanitary Officer.	

2449 Wt. W14957/M90 750,000 1/16 J.B.C. & A. Forms/C.2118/12.

WAR DIARY
or
INTELLIGENCE SUMMARY

(Erase heading not required.)

Army Form C. 2118.

Place	Date	Hour	Summary of Events and Information	Remarks and references to Appendices
BAILLEUL	July 30/16	10 a.m.	Visited 1st/1/10th Field Ambulance and saw their Sanitary arrangements which were satisfactory.	
"	"	3 p.m.	Visited the 105th Field Ambulance & saw their Sanitary arrangements which were satisfactory.	
NORTE PIP Camp	July 31/16	11 a.m.	Visited KORTE PIP Camp with Sanitary Officer 2nd Army, the camp is still far from satisfactory regarding nothing. Reported to D.D.M.S. 36th Division.	
Red July	"	12 p.m.	Inspected Camp at Red Lodge, proper latrine, refuse disposal, also the Camp required cleaning up, arranged with the M.O.S there. None the less immediate.	
Westhof Farm	"	2.30 p.m.	Visited WESTHOF FARM with Sanitary Officer 2nd Army, the sanitary conditions here were satisfactory.	
BAILLEUL	"	4.30 p.m.	Visited 108th Field Ambulance with Sanitary Officer 2nd Army, the sanitary conditions were very satisfactory.	

36th (Ulster) Divn.

"Confidential"
August 1916

War Diary
of
O. C. 76th Sanitary Section

August 1916

Army Form C. 2118.

WAR DIARY
or
INTELLIGENCE SUMMARY
(Erase heading not required.)

Place	Date	Hour	Summary of Events and Information	Remarks and references to Appendices
KORTE-PYP	1/9/16	10/30 a.m.	Inspected KORTEPYP Camp with D.A.D.M.S 36th Division and arranged with the M.O.'s the to have further sanitary arrangements carried out.	
ALDERSHOT HUTS	"	11/30 a.m.	Inspected Sanitary arrangements of Anzac Exhibition Battalion at Aldershot Huts. If the NEUVE EGLISE Road and arranged for conveying fine bags to be made & attached to field kitchens of the forward gun keeps which are most insanitary there among with.	
RED LODGE	"	2/30 p.m.	Visited Red LODGE Camp with D.A.D.M.S 36th Division and arranged with the M.O.'s there to have fly proof latrines made & also urine pits.	
DRANOUTRE	"	11/30 a.m.	Visited the water supply at DRANOUTRE with D.A.D.M.S 36th Division to look over charge of the water supply.	
BAILLEUL	"	5 p.m.	Visited the Sanitary Section Camp at BAILLEUL with D.A.D.M.S 36th Division and showed him all models of Sanitary appliances which have been erected by my unit	

Army Form C. 2118.

WAR DIARY
or
INTELLIGENCE SUMMARY

(Erase heading not required.)

Instructions regarding War Diaries and Intelligence Summaries are contained in F. S. Regs., Part II. and the Staff Manual respectively. Title Pages will be prepared in manuscript.

Place	Date	Hour	Summary of Events and Information	Remarks and references to Appendices
BAILLEUL	Aug 2/16	10/30 a.m.	The A.D.M.S. 86th Division visited the Sanitary Section Camp and inspected the models. Plan of latrines, urinals, field kitchen with expedient grease trap, field oven, ablution benches & room ventilators. All display of empty tins.	
"	"	11/30 a.m.	Grave of chinese coolie been found in the mid² from the field line. I visited the B.D.M.S. V Corps with a view to having the hole examined by a water specialist.	
NEUVE EGLISE	"	12/30 p.m.	Visited the Divisional Baths on the NEUVE EGLISE Road with the A.D.M.S. 36th Division. Dry forms latrines, purpose incinerator, and arrangements for kitchen wash packing.	
"	"	1 p.m.	Visited Cemetery. Park on NEUVE EGLISE Road. The present grease pits must be filled in and a field kitchen with expedient grease trap made, also all the latrine must be proved and the incinerator moved properly building.	

WAR DIARY
or
INTELLIGENCE SUMMARY

(Erase heading not required.)

Army Form C. 2118.

Place	Date	Hour	Summary of Events and Information	Remarks and references to Appendices
NEUVE EGLISE	2/8/16	2/30 p.m.	Inspected Sanitary arrangements of 167 Coy R.E. Latrines must be made fly proof; time must be a proper pit dug for urinal, ash bins, buckets etc. must be cleaned up in the Camp.	
ROMA-RIN	"	3/30 p.m.	Visited Collecting Post at ROMARIN, a new site had to be approved by Corps H.Q. No advice	
BAILLEUL	"	4/45 p.m.	Inspected Sanitary arrangements of 110th Field Ambulance which were very satisfactory.	
BAILLEUL	3/8/16	11/30 a.m.	Visited H.Q. Divisional Train at BAILLEUL and saw the Sanitary arrangements, ordered latrines to be made fly proof, & proper urine pit to be made and evaporating grease trap.	
"	"	12/30 p.m.	Visited 8th Cameron Highld Laundry and saw the O.C. about nothing of value from medical contn.	

WAR DIARY
or
INTELLIGENCE SUMMARY
(Erase heading not required.)

Army Form C. 2118.

Instructions regarding War Diaries and Intelligence Summaries are contained in F.S. Regs., Part II. and the Staff Manual respectively. Title Pages will be prepared in manuscript.

Place	Date	Hour	Summary of Events and Information	Remarks and references to Appendices
BAILLEUL	3/8/16	2/30 p.m.	Visited No 1 Section Divisional Train. I am then sanitary arrangements a new urine pit requires to be dug. I found they were making new latrines but of a bad pattern as they were not fly proof. W.U.R. to inspect gas latrines erected on model at 76 F.Amby. Such in Camps. A field kitchen with an expanding grease trap requires rechecking.	
"	"	3/30 p.m.	Visited No 3 Coy Divisional Train. Saw sanitary arrangements. Fly proof latrine, evaporating grease trap and new urine pit requires renewing.	
"	"	4/30 p.m.	Visited No 4 Coy Divisional Train. The fly proof latrine of this Coy were very satisfactory, as were all the sanitary arrangements.	
"	"	5/30 p.m.	Visited No 2 Coy Divisional Train. All their sanitary arrangements were of a very satisfactory nature.	

Army Form C. 2118.

WAR DIARY
or
INTELLIGENCE SUMMARY
(Erase heading not required.)

Instructions regarding War Diaries and Intelligence Summaries are contained in F. S. Regs., Part II. and the Staff Manual respectively. Title Pages will be prepared in manuscript.

Place	Date	Hour	Summary of Events and Information	Remarks and references to Appendices
NEUVE EGLISE	Jan 4/8/16	11 a.m.	Jan 16 R.D.R. Pinero at Hopre EGLISE, arranged with Second in Command to order the found Latrines, urine pits & defecating heaps, abolition trench mental latrines. Saw M.O. who was out. Left these subjects for O.i/c. printed on labels no orders is not to disinfect in.	
BAILLEUL	5/8/16	10/30 a.m.	Arrived at the Sanitary arrangements at the 36th Divisional Specialist School, and anti-gas school.	
WESTHOF FARM	"	11/45 a.m.	Inspected new Sanitary arrangements 1/c M.M.P. tablets found every day in good order	
"	"	1.45 p.m.	Reported O.C. 36th Divisional Supply Coy to the 2nd and 35th Divisions for being made no attempt to carry out Army sanitary arrangements at his camp at WESTHOF FARM.	
FLETRE	"	3 p.m.	Inspected the Divisional Supply Column's Sanitary arrangements which were excellent.	

2449 Wt. W14957/Mgo 750,000 1/16 J.B.C. & A. Forms/C.2118/12.

WAR DIARY
or
INTELLIGENCE SUMMARY

(Erase heading not required.)

Army Form C. 2118.

Place	Date	Hour	Summary of Events and Information	Remarks and references to Appendices
MONT NOIR	6/8/1916	9/30 a.m.	Nothing to report.	
BAILLEUL	7/8/16	7 a.m.	My unit moved from MONT. NOIR. to new quarters in BAILLEUL. Arranged to have models of sanitary appliances erected in the Camp.	
DRANOUTRE	"	2 p.m.	Inspected Divisional Baths & arranged for new sanitary appliances to be erected.	
"	"	5 p.m.	Saw Sanitary arrangements at 110th Field Ambulance advanced Dressing Post.	
BAILLEUL	8/8/16	9/30 a.m.	Capt Pierre Rame reported for duty as Assistant Sanitary Officer	
"	"	10 a.m.	Sent Corpl Durkin of my unit to supervise the erection of an Incinerator for burning excreta at WEST HOF FARM	
"	"	10/30 a.m.	Inspected all mobile stables of the Division received area.	

Army Form C. 2118.

WAR DIARY
or
INTELLIGENCE SUMMARY

(Erase heading not required.)

Instructions regarding War Diaries and Intelligence Summaries are contained in F. S. Regs., Part II. and the Staff Manual respectively. Title Pages will be prepared in manuscript.

Place	Date	Hour	Summary of Events and Information	Remarks and references to Appendices
NEUVE EGLISE ROAD.	8/6/16	2 p.	Inspected Sanitary arrangements at 36th Div. Ordnance Dump & arranged to have a cupboard & cupboard erected & new sanitary appliances.	
BAILLEUL	9/6/16	6/30	Inspected sanitary arrangements of Divisional Specialist School & advised new sanitary appliances.	
"	"	10:30 am	Inspected Sanitary arrangements of 7th, 9th, 10th & 11th Leinster Battalions which are very satisfactory.	
KORTE-PYP Camp	"	2 p.m.	Inspected KORTEPYP CAMP and saw new sanitary appliances which I had to erected by the various units there; these were on the whole satisfactory.	

WAR DIARY
or
INTELLIGENCE SUMMARY

(Erase heading not required.)

Army Form C. 2118.

Place	Date	Hour	Summary of Events and Information	Remarks and references to Appendices
KORTE-PYP.	10/9/16	10/30 a.m.	Inspected & saw Sanitary arrangements of the 8th & 1st E. Yorkshire Battalions which we are relieving.	
"	"	11/30 a.m.	Inspected new Sanitary arrangements of 36th Div Field Ambulance rear Schopedruy.	
TRENCHES	"	2 p.	The Sanitary arrangements of the 15th Royal Irish Rifles and 11th Royal Irish Rifles are satisfactory.	
BAILLEUL	11/9/16	9/30 a.m.	The Sanitary works at Sanitary Section BAILLEUL are now complete.	
"	"	10/30 a.m.	The Sanitary arrangements at Ordnance Depot were inspected & found satisfactory.	

WAR DIARY
or
INTELLIGENCE SUMMARY

(Erase heading not required.)

Army Form C. 2118.

Place	Date	Hour	Summary of Events and Information	Remarks and references to Appendices
BAILLEUL	11/5/16	2 p.m.	visited M.O. of 36" Division Train with regard to a can to Grebels which have received was his Camp is a Unknown manner. Saw the Religious Mission about leaving the child concerned.	
NORTE-CYR.	12/5/16	10/30 a.m.	Inspected the Sanitary arrangements of 9th Royal Inniskilling Fusiliers very satisfactory	
"	"	11/30 a.m.	The Sanitary condition of the Camp of the 5th Reg of Irish Rifles requires our attention. C.O. will be interviewed.	
BAILLEUL	"	2 p.m.	Saw Sanitary arrangements of the 4 Coy's Divisional Train which were most satisfactory.	
ROMARIN	13/5/16	10 a.m.	visited water filter at ROMARIN & found under repair in spite of this, ordered filtration to be stopped.	
"	"	11 a.m.	Inspected Sanitary arrangements of 121st Coy R.E. very satisfactory.	

2449 Wt. W14957/M90 750,000 1/16 J.B.C. & A. Forms/C.2118/12.

Army Form C. 2118.

WAR DIARY
or
INTELLIGENCE SUMMARY

(Erase heading not required.)

Instructions regarding War Diaries and Intelligence Summaries are contained in F. S. Regs., Part II. and the Staff Manual respectively. Title Pages will be prepared in manuscript.

Place	Date	Hour	Summary of Events and Information	Remarks and references to Appendices
DRANOU-TRE	13/5/16	2 p.m.	Saw new Sanitary Officers at Advanced Dressing Post. Found everything very satisfactory.	
PETIT-PONT	14/5/16	11 a.m.	Inspected Sanitary arrangements & Camps of 153rd Brigade R.F.A. with A.D.M.S. 86th Division, advised on new sanitary officers being evolved.	
BAILLEUL	15/5/16	10/30 a.m.	Inspected Sanitary arrangements of 53rd Infantry Brigade. Found Latrines under Sanitary Officer BAILLEUL.	
"	"	12 p.m.	Saw Sanitary Arrangements of 173rd Brigade R.F.A. & advised on new officers being made.	
"	"	2 p.m.	Saw M.O. Divisional Train at A.S.C. Dumps and advised that a new sign be built and also an incinerator.	

Army Form C. 2118.

WAR DIARY
or
INTELLIGENCE SUMMARY

(Erase heading not required.)

Instructions regarding War Diaries and Intelligence Summaries are contained in F. S. Regs., Part II. and the Staff Manual respectively. Title Pages will be prepared in manuscript.

Place	Date	Hour	Summary of Events and Information	Remarks and references to Appendices
NEUVE EGLISE	10/6/16	10/30	Inspected Baths & 7th Division at NEUVE EGLISE an ordered Hot food & latrines, proper urine pit & work pit to be made arranged for filled ranks the made for the spread of scrappy meals	
KORTE-PYP	"	"	Inspected Sanitary arrangements of 9th Royal Irish Fusiliers and ordered the proper latrines & temporary urine troughs to be made	
Reek Inely	"	2 pm	Inspected Sanitary arrangements of 14th Royal Irish Rifles and ordered same & previous division to them	
FLETRE	"	3.30 pm	Inspected Divisional Supply Columns Sanitary arrangements found them satisfactory	
BAILLEUL	17/6/16	10/30 am	Inspected 108th Field Ambulance with ADMS 36th Division and found their Sanitary arrangements satisfactory	

WAR DIARY
or
INTELLIGENCE SUMMARY

(Erase heading not required.)

Army Form C. 2118.

Place	Date	Hour	Summary of Events and Information	Remarks and references to Appendices
BAILLEUL	17/8/16	11/30 a.m.	Inspected Sanitary arrangements of 1st Divisional Group School with the Assistant 86th Division and arranged with the Adjutant G.S.R.R. that Sanitary Appliances made and tested be a Engineer Officer 76th Sanitary Section for duty.	
WESTHOF FARM	17/8/16	2 p.m.	Inspected 36th Divisional Signal Coy and found their Sanitary arrangements very bad. Reported to A.D.M.S. 36th Division. Saw Sanitary arrangements of the M.M.P. which were most satisfactory.	
KORTE PYP CAMP	18/8/16	10/30 a.m.	Inspected V.C. Sanitary arrangements of the 108th Machine Gun Coy, 9th Royal Irish Fusiliers, 12th Royal Irish Rifles, 11th Royal Irish Rifles and 13th Royal Irish Rifles, and found Reserve of previously scrutinized with the Sanitary Appliances.	

Army Form C. 2118.

WAR DIARY or INTELLIGENCE SUMMARY
(Erase heading not required.)

Instructions regarding War Diaries and Intelligence Summaries are contained in F. S. Regs., Part II. and the Staff Manual respectively. Title Pages will be prepared in manuscript.

Place	Date	Hour	Summary of Events and Information	Remarks and references to Appendices
St Jans Cappel	19/8/16	10.30 a.m.	Visited the Chateau at St Jans Cappel with the R.E. & O.C. 36th Division Each sought of "M.T. mph", and found the sharers of the room is faulty. Arranged that the Italian to be up and hence to a hostage as Div. HQrs as bivouac in the village of St Jans Cappel. Used to Q head 36th Division as this is right.	
Bailleul	20/8/16	2 p.m. 6 p.m.	Inst. and "sept 3" Chateau at St Jans Cappel and found up required 2 rooms & wooden presses for my fellows to storage it. D.Whert. Report.	
Petit Pont	21/8/16	10.30 a.m. 6 p.m.	9 a.m. 1st Royal Irish Fusiliers took artillery of the 2nd and 1st Essex trailers at H.Qs now in Petit Pont for this. I visited them and found it also impossible for the to tend beds for sick of their section works with the Infantry to explain loppy work for Inventory road.	

Army. Form C. 2118.

WAR DIARY
or
INTELLIGENCE SUMMARY

(Erase heading not required.)

Instructions regarding War Diaries and Intelligence Summaries are contained in F. S. Regs., Part II. and the Staff Manual respectively. Title Pages will be prepared in manuscript.

Place	Date	Hour	Summary of Events and Information	Remarks and references to Appendices
Red Lodge	2/6/16	11/30 a.m.	Visited the camp & saw the sanitary arrangements of the 14th the Purple Guns Rifles and 9th Rl Irish Fusiliers and found their arrangements progressing satisfactorily.	
"	"	2 p.m.	Visited & saw sanitary arrangements at the withdrawing pard of 109th & 110th Ambulance which were satisfactory.	
St Jans Cappel	24/8/16	10/30 a.m.	Visited the Château with officers 36th Division & arranged about latrine urinals horse pits being made.	
BAILLEUL	"	12 pm	Inspected Sanitary arrangements of the 36th Div Troop School and arranged about another latrine from any kind to supervised the sickening & Sanitary Appliances.	
St Jans Cappel	"	2 pm	Inspected all billets in Montkoye in which troops are about to billetted.	

2449 Wt. W14957/M90 750,000 1/16 J.B.C. & A. Forms/C.2118/12.

Army Form C. 2118.

WAR DIARY
or
INTELLIGENCE SUMMARY

(Erase heading not required.)

Instructions regarding War Diaries and Intelligence Summaries are contained in F. S. Regs., Part II. and the Staff Manual respectively. Title Pages will be prepared in manuscript.

Place	Date	Hour	Summary of Events and Information	Remarks and references to Appendices
St Jans Cappel	29/3/16	10.30 a.m.	Visited all billets to be used by troops and all Estaminets in the village that nots from the hands of all children in this billets and Estaminets for the purpose of examining for the Diphtheria bacillus.	
Petit Pan	"	10.30 a.m.	In future the Sanitary arrangements of the HQ's, 10th & 104th Brigades, 121 Coy R.E., 13 Regt 2nd Rifles, 10th Regt Rifles, Infantry Brothers, Cavalry Working parties, and 2nd 2 Coy 36th Divisional train and Field Post Party.	
St Jans Cappel	29/3/16	10.30 a.m.	Having seen the Dr in Sillies this morning I arranged for the Sergeant in charge to follow the work from Rest to our forming through the village.	
Jerdon	"	p.m.	Inspected the new huts occupied by the 10 S. H. & 104th F.B. up to date from its Sanitary arrangements & cleanliness.	

WAR DIARY or INTELLIGENCE SUMMARY

Army Form C. 2118.

Place	Date	Hour	Summary of Events and Information	Remarks and references to Appendices
BAILLEUL	25/9/16	9/30 a.m.	92 inch Trench Mortars of the 61st divn at S. Jans Cappel were all found to be free from the defect in Barillus. The rods fitted by the mortar fitter, Jno Hitchens at S. Jans Cappel was found to be of proper specifications.	
NORTE- PYP CAMP	"	11/30 a.m.	Inspected 70 mm Rd sanitary arrangements of No D 1st, 9, 15, 10, 15 + 75 th Rifles. Mins 2 Rifles and 107 th & 109 th machine gun comp arms to found their sanitary arrangements progressing satisfactorily.	
S.te MARIE CAPPEL	"	6 p.m.	Visited from the sanitary arrangements at R. Buisinet School, arranged to chloride Urinvals, fly proof latrines and fill in unsanitary construction.	

Army Form C. 2118.

Instructions regarding War Diaries and Intelligence Summaries are contained in F. S. Regs., Part II. and the Staff Manual respectively. Title Pages will be prepared in manuscript.

WAR DIARY
or
INTELLIGENCE SUMMARY
(Erase heading not required.)

Place	Date	Hour	Summary of Events and Information	Remarks and references to Appendices
BAILLEUL	26/8/16	10 a.m.	Saw the sanitary arrangements of the 11th Royal Irish Rifles, 10th Royal Innishkillen Fusiliers, Ordnance Dump and Divisional Supply Columns and found them satisfactory.	
St Jans Cappel	27/8/16	10 a.m.	The drains of the Orderlies were all taken up & cleared out and relaid, new fronts placed in the latrines and a new cistern erected in the grounds.	
WESTHOF FARM	"	2 p.m.	Inspected & saw the sanitary arrangements of the 36th MD in hand & supd. Coy which seemed satisfactory, afterwards with ADMS. 36th Division	
BAILLEUL	"	3 p.m.	Saw the sanitary arrangements of the 7 Motor Ambulance Workshop Coy which were most satisfactory.	

Army Form C. 2118.

WAR DIARY
or
INTELLIGENCE SUMMARY
(Erase heading not required.)

Instructions regarding War Diaries and Intelligence Summaries are contained in F. S. Regs., Part II. and the Staff Manual respectively. Title Pages will be prepared in manuscript.

Place	Date	Hour	Summary of Events and Information	Remarks and references to Appendices
Radinghem	28/8/16	10/30 Noon	Saw Veterinary arrangements of the 13th Royal Irish Rifles, 11th Royal Inniskilling Fusiliers, 8th & 10th Royal Irish Rifles and also arrangements for offices of the 109th Field Ambulance. These were satisfactory.	
BAILLEUL	29/8/16	10/30 a.m.	Inspected with the Veterinary officer all the main supplies in the Divisional Area.	
St Jans Cappel	30/8/16	10 a.m.	Visited another billet on Farm & village and both seemed to make for bathing	
NEUVE EGLISE	"	12 p.m.	Saw Veterinary arrangements of the 8 Y.C. & 9th Inniskilling Battalions Special Brigade R.E.'s Gas Coys, 108 Machine gun Coy, 9th Royal Irish Rifles, 14th Royal Irish Rifles and 2nd Inniskilling, 14th Royal Irish Rifles & 9 Inniskilling Battalion and found them satisfactory	

Army Form C. 2118

WAR DIARY
or
INTELLIGENCE SUMMARY
(Erase heading not required.)

Instructions regarding War Diaries and Intelligence Summaries are contained in F.S. Regs., Part II. and the Staff Manual respectively. Title Pages will be prepared in manuscript.

Place	Date	Hour	Summary of Events and Information	Remarks and references to Appendices
MONT NOIR	31/9/16	9/30 a.m.	Sent in Monthly Sanitary Report to the W.D. of 86th Division and saw the Camp Commandant with regard to water supply & water for troops and 31st Jano Coppl.	
BAILLEUL	1/30 p.m.		Saw Veterinary arrangements of 16th Division, Grooms' Schools, a Echelon D.A.C. & H.Q.'s D.A.C., Regimen properly ordering.	
St Jano Cappel	" 2	3 p.m.	Saw 16th Division Commander at the Chateau and discussed the sanitary arrangements which had been carried out there.	

"Confidential"

Sept 1916

140/134

36th Div.

War Diary of Capt. J. Davies. R.A.M.C.

O. C. 76th Sanitary Section

30th September 1916.

> COMMITTEE FOR THE
> MEDICAL HISTORY OF THE WAR
> Date 30 OCT 1915

Army Form C. 2118.

WAR DIARY
or
INTELLIGENCE SUMMARY.
(Erase heading not required.)

Instructions regarding War Diaries and Intelligence Summaries are contained in F. S. Regs., Part II. and the Staff Manual respectively. Title pages will be prepared in manuscript.

Place	Date	Hour	Summary of Events and Information	Remarks and references to Appendices
BAILLEUL	1/9/16	10 a.m.	A.A.M.S. moved his Office from MONT NOIR to BAILLEUL	
S:T JANS CAPPEL	"	"	Inspected wet-supply of S:T JANS CAPPEL. During Visit any inspected the sanitary arrangements of 9th Royal Irish Rifles, 11th Chlrs, 109th Machine Gun Coy, 16th Royal Irish Rifles, 108th Machine Gun Coy, H.Q.s 108th Brigade & 109th Field Amb: Belling.	
PETIT PONT	2/9/16	10 a.m.	Inspected quarters of 107th Brigade, also sans sanitary arrangements of 12th R.E's, 15th Royal Irish Rifles, 150th Coy R.E.	
S:T JANS CAPPEL	3/9/16	10 a.m.	Inspected sanitary arrangements of 36th Divisional H.Q's also Divisional Supply column and Divisional train.	
BAILLEUL	4/9/16	10 a.m.	Inspected Sanitary arrangements of the Mobile Veterinary Section, Divisional Ammunition Column, & Ammunition Subpark, to ProvostKhm Section.	
TROIS ROIS	5/9/16	10 a.m.	Inspected Divisional Baths at TROIS ROIS & DRANOUTRE also Chateau occupied by H.Q's of S:T JANS CAPPEL and saw sanitary arrangements of the 110th Field Ambulance	

WAR DIARY
or
INTELLIGENCE SUMMARY.
(Erase heading not required.)

Army Form C. 2118.

Place	Date	Hour	Summary of Events and Information	Remarks and references to Appendices
WESTHOF FARM	6/9/116	10 a.m.	9 July 15. Sanitary arrangements of Quartier Pilou at WESTHOF FARM also all unit HQrs in the 6 Divisional Area. Also Sanitary arrangements in the trenches occupied by G/K Regt. 2nd Bn Rifles, 11 Regt. 2nd 2 Rifles, 12th Royal Irish Rifles, 13 Bn Royal Irish Rifles, 15th Royal Irish Rifles, 8th Royal Irish Rifles, & 172 2nd Brigade R.G.A.	
NEUVE EGLISE	7/9/116	10 a.m.	Inspected the sanitary arrangements of 16 & 15th Royal Irish Rifles, R.E. ordnance Dump, Stables at KANDAHAR FARM, also HQrs of the 107th, 108th & 109th VI Brigade.	
DRANOUTRE	8/9/116	10 a.m.	Inspected the sanitary arrangements at Dranoutre Huts, DRANOUTRE 109th Brigade Dranoutre Camp, Divisional School, 21st Coy Ankle in Camp, Trenches, Details & Advanced Dump Station, DRANOUTRE	
STE MARIE CAPPEL	9/9/116	10 a.m.	Inspected sanitary arrangements at the Divisional School STE MARIE CAPPEL the sanitary arrangements of the village of DRANOUTRE and the 167 Coy. R.E.S.	

WAR DIARY
or
INTELLIGENCE SUMMARY.
(Erase heading not required.)

Army Form C. 2118.

Place	Date	Hour	Summary of Events and Information	Remarks and references to Appendices
DRANOU-TRE	16/9/15	10 am	Inspected the Divisional Baths at DRANOUTRE and TROIS ROIS. The sanitary Offr of the 2nd Army inspected the 28 Westminster Sector.	
DRANOU-TRE	19/9/15	10 am	Inspected the Trenches Reinforced and Posts of the 16th Brigade, also the Cerebral Susp: Station at TROIS ROIS. 10 9/15 yoshe, 9th R Rifles, 15th Rifles, 2nd R Rifles, 14th Rgd 2nd Rifles, 173 Brigade R.B.B.	
WAKEFERED HDTS	18/9/15	10 am	Inspected Servicer occupied by 11th Royal Irish Rifles, Inskilling, Land A HAR FARM and the Birde Barriers.	
NEUVE EGLISE	19/9/15	10 am	Inspected Trenches No 1 to 107 Brigade and Trench supply of St JANS CAPPEL.	
ST JANS CAPPEL	24/9/15	10 am	Inspected a supplier low of Defellatures in a civila cottage at ST JANS CAPPEL & the trench from its South Regatine.	
	26/9/15	10 am	Inspected Trenches occupied 11th by RB u, 10th & 11th Ambulance, 1st Royal Irish Rifles, 10 u and 18 u Royal Irish Rifles.	
BAILLEUL	18/9/15	10 am	Inspected Sanitary arrangements of the Divisional Ammunition Column and Divisional Supply Column.	

WAR DIARY
or
INTELLIGENCE SUMMARY.
(Erase heading not required.)

Army Form C. 2118.

Place	Date	Hour	Summary of Events and Information	Remarks and references to Appendices
DRANOU-TRE	16/9/16	10 a.m.	Inspected sanitary arrangements of Y.B.C.A Hut at Dranoutre, 16th Royal Irish Rifles, 153rd Brigade R.F.A, 36th Division 5 inch Hy. Battn Divisional Ammunition Column.	
ST JEAN CAPPEL	17/9/16	10 a.m.	Inspected Divisional Headquarters also Divisional Baths and made enquiry.	
LOCRE	18/9/16	10 a.m.	Inspected The Sanitary arrangements to Divisional Ammunition Column, 5th Cavalry Division, Jung Schule and 17th Schützen School.	
MONT NOIR	19/9/16	10 a.m.	The Château at Mont NOIR being taken over as an Officers' ex Station. The sanitary arrangements were inspected, also the ground occupied by 125, 10th Inf Brigade.	
KEMMEL	20/9/16	10 a.m.	Drove up to ST JEAN CAPPEL via KEMMEL, Lindenhoek, Mont NOIR and ST JANS CAPPEL men inspected.	

Army Form C. 2118.

WAR DIARY
or
INTELLIGENCE SUMMARY.
(Erase heading not required.)

Instructions regarding War Diaries and Intelligence Summaries are contained in F. S. Regs., Part II. and the Staff Manual respectively. Title pages will be prepared in manuscript.

Place	Date	Hour	Summary of Events and Information	Remarks and references to Appendices
DRANOU-TRE	2/9/16	10 a.m.	Visited all Cafés & Estaminets at DRANOUTRE and NEUVE EGLISE to ascertain whether pit stove hole for making soup and also how it floors & cups &c in which teas in coffee served to Men's men kept clean	
KORTIPIP CAMP.	22/9/16	10 a.m.	Visited the Divisional Canteen & saw all work taken at the Divisional Area.	
S⁺ MARIE CAPPEL	23/9/16	10 a.m.	Visited the Divisional School at S⁺ MARIE CAPPEL and saw the Sanitary arrangements also the Sanitary arrangements at G.H.Q. 4⁺ Sanitary Section	
DRANOU-TRE	24/9/16	10 a.m.	Visited and saw the Sanitary arrangements of the Brigade occupied by the 109th Brigade	
DRANOU-TRE	25/9/16	10 a.m.	Visited a number of Farm areas DRANOUTRE in which cases of People are being billeted by civilian clerks, also visited the H.Q's of 107th 108th & 109th Brigades.	
BAILLEUL	26/9/16	10 a.m.	Inspected the Sanitary arrangements at Ordnance Dump & Midilary P. Office & saw gas hut at Aircraft Area.	

WAR DIARY
or
INTELLIGENCE SUMMARY.
(Erase heading not required.)

Army Form C. 2118.

Instructions regarding War Diaries and Intelligence Summaries are contained in F. S. Regs., Part II. and the Staff Manual respectively. Title pages will be prepared in manuscript.

Place	Date	Hour	Summary of Events and Information	Remarks and references to Appendices
KANDAHAR FARM	7/9/16	10 am	Visited Dumps of 107th Brigade and old regimental aid posts etc.	
DRANOUTRE	8/9/16	10 am	Visited Divisional Baths at DRANOUTRE and NEUVE EGLISE ROAD, saw about 30 pill-boxes on new hills NEUVE EGLISE & DRANOUTRE	
MONT NOIR	9/9/16	10 am	A car of Senior medical officers arrived at the Officers Rest Station, MONTNOIR. Visited them & saw the O/C with regard to their future etc.	
STINKING FARM	10/9/16	10 am	Inspected Dumps of 10th Brigade and saw the regimental aid posts; also saw hills of DRANOUTRE and NEUVE EGLISE	

Confidential.

36th Divn
149/1815

Oct 1916 Vol 11

War Diary
of
Capt J. Davies, R.A.M.C
O.C. 76th Sanitary Section.

31st October 1916.

COMMITTEE FOR THE
MEDICAL HISTORY OF THE WAR
Date 9 DEC. 1916

WAR DIARY
or
INTELLIGENCE SUMMARY.
(Erase heading not required.)

Army Form C. 2118.

Place	Date	Hour	Summary of Events and Information	Remarks and references to Appendices
BAILLEUL	Oct 1 1916	10am	D.o Sanitary inspects at Shackhill Huts, Derry Huts, 11½ Jabou Batteries and No 17 Cafe aircraft. Billets were inspected.	
BAILLEUL	Oct 2 1916	10am	D.o filter beds being erected at Starkhill Huts & Derry Huts were inspected and the sanitary arrangements of the 167th & 150 Coy R.E. were inspected also those of the Military Police, Divisional HQ's, HQ's RA, 8 Bn of the Cheshires, Batteries and Divisional Huts.	
BAILLEUL	Oct 3 1916	10am	D.o sanitary arrangements of the Divisional Guard School, 14th Royal Irish Rifles, 9th Royal Irish Rifles, 14th Royal Irish Rifles Transport lines, 10th Inniskilling Dragoons, 11th Inniskillings, Buet Noir, 10 Inniskilling Fusiliers, 11th Inniskilling Fusiliers were inspected.	
BAILLEUL	Oct 4 1916	10am	A sanitary inspection of the farm containing Div Supply Column, was carried out, also of the 110th Field Ambulance, a number of billets in the Divisional Area were also seen.	
BAILLEUL	Oct 5 1916	10am	A sanitary inspection of R. H. Q's Divisional Area, 36th Divisional Ammunition Sub park, Special Early R.E's and Divisional School St MARIE CAPPEL was carried out.	

WAR DIARY
or
INTELLIGENCE SUMMARY.
(Erase heading not required.)

Army Form C. 2118.

Place	Date	Hour	Summary of Events and Information	Remarks and references to Appendices
BAILLEUL	6/6		9th Seaforths amalgamate to be 12 & 14 Royal Irish Rifles & 2nd Regt	
	1916	10 a.m.	Divis Invd was 108 Brderies for bring 11th Royal Irish Rifles, 13 &	
			Royal Irish Rifles, 107th Brigade HQ's were down	
BAILLEUL	6/10	10 am	95d mob Inft of Jr. JAS CAPPER was down the territory	
	1916		and part of HQ's 108th, 109th Brigades, 172 Brigade R.F.	
BAILLEUL	8/10		36th Division 2nd in T 122 Eng R.E's was told	
	1916	10 am	Outward Evening Station etc LINDENHOEK inspected.	
BAILLEUL	9/10	10 am	9th Sanitary Officer 36th Division proceeded in 10 days leave to	
	1916		England	
BAILLEUL	10/10		Military Inspection	
	1916			
Bailleul	11/10/16		Military Inspection	
BAILLEUL	12/10/16		Military Inspection	
BAILLEUL	13/10/16		Military Inspection	
BAILLEUL	14/10/16		Military Inspection	
BAILLEUL	15/10/16		Military Inspection	

WAR DIARY
or
INTELLIGENCE SUMMARY.
(Erase heading not required.)

Army Form C. 2118.

Instructions regarding War Diaries and Intelligence Summaries are contained in F. S. Regs., Part II. and the Staff Manual respectively. Title pages will be prepared in manuscript.

Place	Date	Hour	Summary of Events and Information	Remarks and references to Appendices
BAILLEUL	16/10/16	10 a.m.	The sanitary arrangements of WESTHOF FARM and billets & baths in DRANOUTRE area were inspected.	
BAILLEUL	17/10/1916	10 a.m.	In advanced dressing station and regimental aid posts at LINDENHOEK were inspected by the ADMS 36th Division.	
BAILLEUL	18/10/1916	10 a.m.	Inspection of KANDAHAR FARM, where troops of DRANOUTRE & WESTHOF FARM & 110th Field Ambulance were carried out.	
BAILLEUL	19/10/1916	10 a.m.	92 Command. NOUVEAU MOND lately placed out of bounds in account, it is now then with arrangements for proper cleaning of same.	
BAILLEUL	20/10/1916	10 a.m.	The ADMS inspected the 110th Field Ambulance.	
"		1 p.m.	The DDMS 36th Division proceeded on leave to England.	
BAILLEUL	21/10/1916	10 a.m.	The sanitary arrangements of Divisional HQs, Divisional Supply Column & the water supply of SANS CAPPEL were seen.	
BAILLEUL	22/10/1916	10 a.m.	The ADMS & Sanitary Officer 36th Division visited New RE sanitary arrangements at the Divisional School Ste MARIE CAPPEL	

WAR DIARY or INTELLIGENCE SUMMARY

Army Form C. 2118.

Place	Date	Hour	Summary of Events and Information	Remarks and references to Appendices
BAILLEUL	23/10 1916	10a.m.	O.C. fill huts at Shankill Huts were less than ½ the R.E. scale & for retain. The sanitary arrangements after inspection of 153 & 173 Brigade R.E. were inadequate.	
BAILLEUL	24/10 1916	10a.m.	O.C. sanitary arrangements at Derry Huts, 13th Royal Irish Rifles, 36th Division Hillsboro', March Retrenchment, Jesuits' Monastery.	
BAILLEUL	25/10 1916	10a.m.	O.C. returned during visits to R.A.P.'s at Kandahar Farm & STINKING FARM were visited. The sanitary arrangements of 150 Coy R.E. & 14th Royal Irish Rifles were inspected.	
BAILLEUL	26/10 1916	10a.m.	O.C. chewing inspection at 110 Coy R.E. and at PETIT PONT were inspected. Re A.D.M.S. Sanitary Offices and Sanitary Offices of the 36th Division.	
BAILLEUL	27/10 1916	10a.m.	O.C. A.D.M.S. & Sanitary Officer 36th Division inspected the camp at SHANKHILL HUTS and also the 104th & 110th Sub Ambulances.	
BAILLEUL	28/10 1916	10a.m.	O.C. A.D.M.S. Sanitary Officer 36th Division inspected DERRY HUTS and Mr Baths. Also the NEUVE EGLISE Road.	

WAR DIARY
or
INTELLIGENCE SUMMARY.
(Erase heading not required.)

Army Form C. 2118.

Place	Date	Hour	Summary of Events and Information	Remarks and references to Appendices
BAILLEUL	29/10/1916		Military Transport	
BAILLEUL	30/10/1916	a.m.	The advanced Dumping Stations at DRANOUTRE and LINDENHOEK were inspected. Transport arrangements H.Q. Units, & 36th Divisional Signal Coy were inspected.	
BAILLEUL	31/10/1916	a.m.	92 Infantry Brigade Groups Stations at KANDAHAR FARM & TROIS RUIS were inspected. The dressing arrangements of Battalions of Bde 11th Royal Irish Rifles, 18th Royal Irish Rifles, 13th Royal Irish Rifles, 9th Royal Irish Regt, 2nd Inniskilling, 13th Royal Irish Rifles, 10th Royal Irish Rifles, 107th Trench Mortar Battery & 121st Coy R.E.'s were seen.	
"	"	3 p.m.	92nd 110th Field Ambulance was inspected.	

No. 10/16

Confidential   36th Divn.

140/86k

WDE12

War Diary

of

Capt J. Davies, R.A.M.C

O. C. 76th Sanitary Section

November 1916.

COMMITTEE FOR THE
MEDICAL HISTORY OF THE WAR
Date -3 JAN. 1917

WAR DIARY
or
INTELLIGENCE SUMMARY.
(Erase heading not required.)

Army Form C. 2118.

Instructions regarding War Diaries and Intelligence Summaries are contained in F.S. Regs., Part II. and the Staff Manual respectively. Title pages will be prepared in manuscript.

Place	Date	Hour	Summary of Events and Information	Remarks and references to Appendices
BAILLEUL	Mon 1/1/15	10 a.m.	Inspected the Sanitary arrangements & saw the drainage system of the following Camps. Div Supply Column, No 1 & No 3 Coy Div Train. No 3 Section D.A.C.	
"	Tues 2/1/15	10 a.m.	Inspected the Sanitary arrangements & saw the drainage system of the following Camps, 150 Coy R.E. Transport lines B 14 R.I. Rifles. Advanced Dressing Station DRANOUTRE	
"	Wed 3/1/15	10 a.m.	Inspected the Sanitary arrangements & drainage of DERRY CAMP, 12 Welsh Fus' Sanitary work. Ablution huts are broken down. 9th 150" 1 Coy R.E. have been asked to repair them. An Officer will have to report in the Camp & more drainage requires cutting in regard to Div H.Q.s, School, Jardin. Inspected Sanitation & drainage of Div H.Q', School, Jardin. 36th Div Sig'al Coy Sanitation school Jardin, more drainage is required.	
"	Thurs 4/1/15	10 a.m.	drills African Bat Stretcher MONT NOIR. Sanitation very good. Inspected sanitary arrangements & saw the drainage of the Camps of the 10 & 109th & 110 #Field Ambulances. very school Jardin	

Army Form C. 2118.

WAR DIARY
or
INTELLIGENCE SUMMARY.
(Erase heading not required.)

Instructions regarding War Diaries and Intelligence Summaries are contained in F. S. Regs., Part II. and the Staff Manual respectively. Title pages will be prepared in manuscript.

Place	Date	Hour	Summary of Events and Information	Remarks and references to Appendices
BAILLEUL	Nov 5/15	10 a.m.	Inspected sanitation & saw drainage of Camps of 11th R.I.Rifles & 13th R.I.Rifles. Sanitation satisfactory. Drainage progressing. 11th Labour Battalion ditto.	
BAILLEUL	Nov 6/15	10 a.m.	10th & 11th Machine Gun Coy. Manure should be taken further away from Camp. Inspected sanitation & saw drainage of Camps of 9th R.I. Rifles, 12th R.I. Rifles, 8th R.I. Rifle, 10th R.I. Rifles. Rampulform. A good deal of drainage is required in these Camps. This is progressing. 121st Coy. R.E. ditto.	
BAILLEUL	Nov 7/15	10 a.m.	Inspected KANDAHAR FARM. Sanitation front. Advanced Dressing Station TROIS ROIS ditto. 167 A.T. Coy. R.E. The filling in of ... under ... repairs. Division Baths - NEUVE EGLISE Road. Sanitation good. Drainage of Camp progressing.	
BAILLEUL	Nov 8/15	10 a.m.	Inspected Divisional Group School. Sanitation satisfactory. Drainage of Camp progressing. Divisional School ST MARIE CAPPEL. Sanitation & drainage very good. Divisional Reinforcement Camp STEENWERCK. Work progressing satisfactorily.	

T.J.34. Wt. W708-776. 500,000. 4/15. Sir J.C. & S.

WAR DIARY
or
INTELLIGENCE SUMMARY.
(Erase heading not required.)

Army Form C. 2118.

Place	Date	Hour	Summary of Events and Information	Remarks and references to Appendices
BALLEUL	Nov 9/16	10 a.m.	Inspected sanitary arrangements & drainage of Aldershot Huts- 3rd Special Brigade R.E.'s. Inspected Huts & Shackwill Huts. Sanitation's satisfactory. Drainage of Camps to be improved.	
"	Nov 10/16	10 a.m.	Inspected Dranker of 10th R. Fusrs Brigade. Sanitation satisfactory, also Jacking Bulford Camp. 2 winter huts approaching and fowl-proof huts regain attention. Drains near the dock house, a new latrine requires attention, bath in the camp and drainage of Camp requires attention.	
"	Nov 11/16	10 a.m.	KORTEY PYR Camp, a latrine at N.E. corner of Camp requires attention. Hy find of the drainage of the Camp requires attention. HQ's Div Amn Column Chemin Sanitation & drainage satisfactory. 107 Ur Armd Raulrs Belling, a new kitchen requires hardening. Hys upon Hy bring between huts, else in attention trench. 107 Ur Machine Gun Coy. A good deal of drainage is required in the Camp.	
"	Nov 12/16	10 a.m.	Inspected RED LODGE, sanitation of the Camp greatly improved and the drainage is progressing satisfactorily. C. Bulley 17th Bgde Wayne Lewis satisfactory 11th Islam Battalion satisfactory	

WAR DIARY
or
INTELLIGENCE SUMMARY.
(Erase heading not required.)

Army Form C. 2118.

Place	Date	Hour	Summary of Events and Information	Remarks and references to Appendices
BAILLEUL	Nov 13/16	10 am	Inspected sanitation at H.Q's Coy 36th Division. 36th Sig. Coy ST JANS CAPPEL H.Q's R.E 36th Division & water supply ST JANS CAPPEL	
"	Nov 14/16	10 am	Inspected Sanitary arrangements of C. Battery, 153rd Brigade R.F.A. Sanitation food, clothing, equipment. D. Battery 173rd Brigade R.F.A. ditto. 20 Coy Army Troops R.E., 121st Coy R.E. 36th Div. Holding Coy.	
"	Nov 15/16	10 am	Inspected C. Section D.A.C. D. Section D.A.C. 130th Battery R.G.A. Military Police WESTHOF FARM. DETTINGEN HUTS. C Battery 172nd Brigade R.F.A.	
"	Nov 16/16	10 am	Inspected Divisional Reinforcement Camp STEINWERCK with the A.D.M.S 36th Division. STINKING FARM & R.A.P.'s near Rectn. Tanks	
"	Nov 17/16	10 am	Divisional Water Supply men inspected. Inspected No 1, 2, 3 & 4 Sections Divisional Train and Transport Lewis of 11th, 12th & 13th Royal Irish Rifles and 9th Royal Irish Fusiliers.	
"	Nov 18/16	10 am	Inspected H.Q's of 108th & 109th Brigades. H.Q's Div Amm Column & B. Section Div. Amm Column & Mobile Vet Section.	

WAR DIARY
or
INTELLIGENCE SUMMARY.
(Erase heading not required.)

Army Form C. 2118.

Place	Date	Hour	Summary of Events and Information	Remarks and references to Appendices
B MILLEUL	Nov 18/15	10 a.m.	Inspected A.D.S. TROIS ROIS and at DRANOUTRE, also the Divisional Baths at NEUVE EGLISE & DRANOUTRE.	
"	Nov 19/15	10 a.m.	Inspected C Battery 153 Bdy R.F.A., S2 Siege Battery, & S McEnketehing Bulletin.	
"	Nov 19/15	10 a.m.	Inspected Wakefield Huts, sanitation of Jacking, drawings of Camp.	
"	Nov 20/15	10 a.m.	Boyourning Derry Camp, filled-in web working now satisfactory. Inspected B. Battery 172nd Brigade R.F.A., HQ's Coy 36th Division,	
"	Nov 21/15	10 a.m.	HQ's R.E. 36th Division & 36th Div Supply Coy ST JANS CAPPEL. Attached conference of Sanitary Officers of Divisions in 2nd Army.	
"	Nov 22/15	10 a.m.	Visited Church Army Hut at KORTYPYP CAMP and advised on sanitary arrangements before made there.	
"	Nov 23/15	10 a.m.	Visited with D.D.M.S. & D.A.D.M.S. IVth Corps. RED LODGE, KORTYPYP CAMP, BULFORD CAMP, SHANKHILL HUTS, DERRY CAMP, and K.X.Y.Z. Iwand Mortar Batteries NEUVE EGLISE.	
"	Nov 24/15	10 a.m.	Nothing to report.	

WAR DIARY or INTELLIGENCE SUMMARY

Army Form C. 2118.

Place	Date	Hour	Summary of Events and Information	Remarks and references to Appendices
BAILLEUL	Nov 25/16	10 a.m.	Inspected 9th Royal Innskilling Fusiliers at Locheport Huts, Sanitation from schgarden, cook dressing. Irrender the addition tents should be enlarged.	
"	Nov 26/16	12 p.m.	Saw Brigadier G. S. [?] & 109th Brigade.	
"	"	10	Attended Conference of ADMS's & Sanitary Officers of the IX Corps at HQ's IX Corps. President ADMS IX Corps.	
"	Nov 26/16	6 p.m.	Inspected the HQ's lines & 36th Div Sigl Coy at S. Jans Cappel.	
"	"	2 p.m.	Saw A.D.M.S. 36th Div & Officers RAMC Stations, MONT NOIR	
"	Nov 27/16	10 a.m.	Proceeded to Officers RAMC Station, MONT NOIR to do duty for the day, for Captain Evans RAMC who was gone overseas into a Court Martial at HAZEBROUCK.	
"	Nov 28		Inspected the Sanitary arrangements & dressings of MC [?]new point lining of the 9th Royal Innskilling Fusiliers, 14 V Royal Inish Rifles, 18th Royal Innskilling Fusiliers & 11th Royal Innskilling Fusiliers.	
"	Nov 28/16			
"	Nov 29/16	0 a.m.	Visited ADMS IX Corps to his officers in question of Sanitary relating	

WAR DIARY
or
INTELLIGENCE SUMMARY.

Place	Date	Hour	Summary of Events and Information	Remarks and references to Appendices
BAILLEUL	Nov 30/16	10 a.c.	Inspected the sanitary arrangements of Camps of 2nd Army A.S.C., No 3 Coy A.S.C., 150 Coy R.E., 221 Coy R.E., and 16th Royal Irish Rifles.	

Army Form C. 2118

WAR DIARY
or
INTELLIGENCE SUMMARY
(Erase heading not required.)

Place	Date	Hour	Summary of Events and Information	Remarks and references to Appendices
BAILLEUL	30/10	10 a.m.	On Arrival The Service Company intercepted & was dressing of Croops to Bn 4 Coy Rly, Bn 3 Coy Engr, 150 Coy R.E., 131 Coy R.E. and 1C Imperial Bors Regt.	

Confidential 6 Ds. 13
Dec 1916   Indices Vol 15

War Diary

of

Capt E. Sprawson R.A.M.C.

O.C. 76th Sanitary Section

31st December 1916.

COMMITTEE FOR THE
MEDICAL HISTORY OF THE WAR
Date 31 JAN. 1917

Army Form C. 2118.

WAR DIARY
or
INTELLIGENCE SUMMARY

(Erase heading not required.)

Instructions regarding War Diaries and Intelligence Summaries are contained in F. S. Regs., Part II. and the Staff Manual respectively. Title Pages will be prepared in manuscript.

Place	Date	Hour	Summary of Events and Information	Remarks and references to Appendices
BAILLEUL	1.12.16		Inspected 108 & 109 Field Ambulances 1A, B & C 172 Brigade Waggon Lines Q&A.	
	2.12.16		Inspection of trucks at WAKEFIELD Huts, MONNOUTH camp and transport Lines. Trunk of 169 Bgde.	
	3.12.16		Inspected WESTHOF in morning and 2 IX Corps Officers Rest Station.	
	4.12.16		Inspected DRANOUTRE baths, 109 FA, AFS, and Divisional School of Instruction at ST MARIE CAPPEL.	
	5.12.16		Inspection at BULFORD, WORTEPP camps and NEUVE EGLISE baths.	
	6.12.16		No 2 Co. AC Divisional train, 36 Div. Supply Co. ASC & No 4 Co. ASC Div. train.	
	7.12.16		Inspection of Red LODGE & HYDE PARK camps and SHANKHILL huts	
	8.12.16		Met new officer staffs over 76 San. Sec. and inspection of 109 & 110 Field Ambulances.	
	9.12.16		Inspection 110 Field Ambulance + 36 DAC HQ. Weekly Sanitary report.	

Army Form C. 2118.

WAR DIARY
or
INTELLIGENCE SUMMARY.
(Erase heading not required.)

Instructions regarding War Diaries and Intelligence Summaries are contained in F.S. Regs., Part II. and the Staff Manual respectively. Title pages will be prepared in manuscript.

Place	Date	Hour	Summary of Events and Information	Remarks and references to Appendices
Bailleul	10.12.16		Took over San See 76, 36 (West) Division from Capt. J. Davies R.Am.C. Clerical work going through weekly reports of units — in afternoon — rode to WESTOUTRE to interview O.C. San See 16 Div. re Sanitary Appliances required in his area. Rode WESTOUTRE back via Croix de Lettre.	
"	11.12.16		With A.D.M.S. to Rufus Camp Prototype Camp. Inspected bath, also bath in afternoon to BAILLEUL Dysentery Hosp. about Scarlet Fever cases from 15 R.D.R. — Late to WAKEFIELD Camp to see M.O. of 15 R.D.R. about Segregation of Contacts. Office work.	
"	12.12.16		Car to 108 Bde H.Q. Inspector of 118 Bde H.Q. Transport lines of 12 R.D.R. 105 M.G.C. 13 R.D.R. 105 M.G.C. to see 108 M.G.C. & new Coy of 11 R.D.R. to R. Inum Stn. Rela Lodge to see Ulster camp. — Office work.	
"	13.12.16		With A.D.M.S. Inspected camps of 36 Sav. H.Q. Sav. B/Echelon, Horn lines of 108 F.A. 109 F.A. & Ulster Veterinary Section. Office work.	
"	14.12.16		Rode with A.D.M.S. to visit Dismounted bath, advanced dressing station 109 F.A. C.172 Battery R.F.A. Howitzer waggon lines, in afternoon car to ST MARIE CAPPEL to 36 Division School of Instruction — inspected it.	

WAR DIARY
or
INTELLIGENCE SUMMARY.
(Erase heading not required.)

Army Form C. 2118.

Place	Date	Hour	Summary of Events and Information	Remarks and references to Appendices
BAILLEUL	15.12.16		With ADMS to inspect No 2 Co ASC Div train, 36 Div Supply column A.T.C. No 4 Co ASC Div train, 36 Div dump & No 1 Co ASC Div train. In afternoon to 8th Entrenching Batt's re isolation of Scarlet fever case, inspected camp also camp of 16 R.I.R. transport lines.	
"	16.12.16.		With ADMS to inspect RED LODGE, 108 M.G.C, Catacombs - ennertation with OC 150 Co R.E. about ventilation of CATACOMBES & training new minicoln site	
"	17.12.16.		Rode inspecting divisional area & see camp site and with A Dir S & to MONT. NOIR inspecting 1st Corps officers Rest Station	
"	18.12.16.		to SHANK HILL huts, 9 R I R, and XYZ TM Btys and Batt HQ. NEUVE EGLISE in afternoon ST. JANS CAPPEL to 36 Div Signal Co & Div HQ.	
"	19.12.16		With ADMS inspecting personnel and water tanks Nos. 42, 35, 39, 40, 38. In afternoon to ETTINGEN huts, B.17² Bat, waggon lines, B.153 Bat, waggon lines, A.153 Bat, waggon lines & No. 3 Section T.A.C.	
"	20.12.16		WAKEFIELD huts - 8 R I R, -12 huts occupied by 1st Scarlet fever contacts of 15 R I R, sprayed, scrubbed & white-washed to period of quarantine expired.	

WAR DIARY or INTELLIGENCE SUMMARY

Army Form C. 2118.

Place	Date	Hour	Summary of Events and Information	Remarks and references to Appendices
BAILLEUL	20.12.16 (contd)		L.O.C. R.E.H.Q.F. farm inspected as explained of (letter to Q) – Inspected transport lines of 8 R.I.R, 10 R.I.R, 1st R.I.R, 9 R.I.R.	
"	21.12.16		Inspection with A Stn. S. of 130 Bath. R.G.A. waggon lines 1st Specialist School of Instruction visited – of Gas School hand effected of Instruction in afternoon 121 Field Co. R.E., 173 Bath. waggon lines	
"	22.12.16		Inspection 279 R. Co. R.E. (the uncouth). No 4 A.S.C. Div train and M.G. (name of Divn school) Gas School Specialist noted. In afternoon inspected R. Co. II Lab. Batt. R.F. (Cape Town) C.I. Co. of same unit. 153 Brigade R.F.A. waggon lines. Y 156 Field Co R.E. HQ.	
"	23.12.16		Inspected with A Stn. & R. Co. II Lab. Batt. R.E. – used latrine & canteen myself & made from luenorlite tin (letter to Q about same). R.Co. Special Batt. No 69. R.E. Divisional latrines. Co. Weekly Sanitary report made up.	
"	24.12.16		276 Sanitary Section and with A Stn. S. & W.F. STOUT R.F. to 16 Divn Sans. Sec. Inspection went in 1X Corps Officers Rest Station, Gravet fence huts of 14th Fusiliering Battn disinfected	
"	25.12.16		Christmas day. Plans for reorganisation of Section work got out.	

WAR DIARY
or
INTELLIGENCE SUMMARY.
(Erase heading not required.)

Army Form C. 2118.

Place	Date	Hour	Summary of Events and Information	Remarks and references to Appendices
BAILLEUL	26.12.16		Attendance at IX Corps Water Control Board. Inspection of A Batt, 172 Bde Waggon lines, 9 R. Irish Fus, Transport lines, 11/R. Inniskg. Transport lines.	
"	27.12.16		Inspection at KORTEPYP of Transport lines of 14 R.I.R. and 10 R. Innisks. Inspection at HQ. 107 Brigade HQ. & Brigade Pioneers also of 107 T.M.B. 108 Bde HQ. Arrangements made that latters no water storage & arrangements made that latters no water storage &c.	
"	28.12.16		To KORTEPYP - taffle to be fitted for A Batt, 172 Bde Waggon lines, 109 T.M. Batt, & 9 M.G. Co. inspected also WEST OF farm. Inspection of B.172 Batt, Waggon lines, N.O.1 Section Or Inspection of 48 Institute Vet. Section, 108 F.A. Horse lines, 36 Div Supp. Col A.S.C., & B. II Lab. Batt R.E. Section worked up status this week.	
"	29.12.16		To KORTEPYP - to arrange disinfection of blankets of 109 Brigade twice as scabies is in the division. To C.S.O. of Div Train to arrange supply of coal for disinfector.	
"	31.12.16		To PINCH BOOM and METEREN to effect sanitary arrangements for 12 & 11 R.I.R. who have gone into Winter there	

"Confidential"

War Diary
of
Capt E. Spranson. R.A.M.C
O/c 70th Sanitary Section

31st January 1917.

COMMITTEE FOR THE
MEDICAL HISTORY OF THE WAR
Date 13 MAR. 1917

WAR DIARY
or
INTELLIGENCE SUMMARY
(Erase heading not required.)

Army Form C. 2118.

Instructions regarding War Diaries and Intelligence Summaries are contained in F.S. Regs., Part II. and the Staff Manual respectively. Title pages will be prepared in manuscript.

Place	Date	Hour	Summary of Events and Information	Remarks and references to Appendices
BAILLEUL	1.1.17		To NORTE PYP re Sheet disinfects 500 blankets were being done daily, arrangements being made to disinfect ↑ CATACOMBS, Inspects of 9 AIR camp NORTE PYP, Church Army hut ↑A Batt 172 Bde Waggon Lines and of 36 Div Signal & Divisional H.Q.	
"	2.1.17		Inspects WAKEFIELD HUTS, occupied by H Co 3rd Special Batt RE. 1st RIR transport Lines also transport Lines of 10 RIR & 9 RIR, 1st RIR transport Lines. "Q" (Sgy duty) 9 RIR, and 10CRE Hof farm. "Q" branch with improvised trench ladders, P.B. were taken over for Camp Commdant & posted at Water tanks 41, 39, 42, 35, 40, 138 4th T.U. men returned, Lecture to 1X Corps School of Sanitation.	
"	4.1.17		Inspects of HRS KANDAHAR farm and trenches occupied by 107 Brigade & 49 R Munster. Two in possession to NORTE PYP re Sheet disinfects, Its camp there (1st RIR) and to 1X Corps Scabies Hosp CAESTRE with Abrns in afternoon.	
"	5.1.17		Inspects 36 SAC H.Q., BELEEA SAC, C Co 11 Labour Batt RE, NoI Reft St.A. In afternoon to RED LODGE ↑HYDE PARK CORNER to spray all huts ↑CATACOMBS to creolin preventin.	
"	6.1.17		Inspects C152 Batt, Waggon Lines, RED LODGE ↑HYDE PAR N CORNER, Sprayers finished in afternoon, to Lt Lyft Col re new supply to disinfects ↑ AA rom Q re Sanitation. Wrote Sanitary Report written, certain paid.	

WAR DIARY
or
INTELLIGENCE SUMMARY.
(Erase heading not required.)

Army Form C. 2118.

Place	Date	Hour	Summary of Events and Information	Remarks and references to Appendices
BAILLEUL	7.1.17		To ST JANS CAPPELLE with ADMS, inspected 36 Div Sig.als camp in afternoon conference with Sanitary Officer 16 Div re Scabies prevention & the Sanitary matter.	
"	8.1.17		With ADMS 6 PINCHBOOM and METEREN, inspection of farms occupied on billets by 13 & 11 RIR and in afternoon with S.P.R. from camp commandant to portable incinerators 41, 39, 42, 35 & 40 returning 6 TO. Went round on their tanks.	
"	9.1.17		Inspection V, X, Y, Z. Trench Mortar Batty's. reports on sanitary improvements. also inspection BOLFORD camp 16 RIR transport lines. Lecture to 1st Corps School of Sanitation.	
"	10.1.17		Demonstration at 76 Sanitary Section camp to IX Corps School of Sanitation and tour of 36 Division camps with them. Token berg Disinfected 107 Regt. Inspected 3 & 173 Battys R.F.A. & 153 Batty. R.F.A. Change in reorganisation of 70 Sanitary Section carried out. Inspected 6th Rekeeping Battn., A.S.C. Divisional dump, No 1 Co M.G. Co, A.S.C.	
"	11.1.17		Inspected No 2 Co M.C. Sec. Train. 3rd Canadian Tunnelling Co., No 4 Co A.S.C. Div. Train Advanced Dressing Station TROIS ROIS, PALMER Lottie, Inoculation re 3rd Disinfector of 107 Regt. at NORTERYP. Inspected A152 Batty. Major Lines, No 3 Sect. S.A.C. Lecture at 9nd School of Sanitation 3 MARIE, CAPPELLE.	
"	12.1.17			

Army Form C. 2118.

WAR DIARY
or
INTELLIGENCE SUMMARY.
(Erase heading not required.)

Instructions regarding War Diaries and Intelligence Summaries are contained in F.S. Regs., Part II. and the Staff Manual respectively. Title pages will be prepared in manuscript.

Place	Date	Hour	Summary of Events and Information	Remarks and references to Appendices
BAILLEUL	13.1.17		To WEST of Farm boring Sanitary NCOs, inspected MDS. BRANDHOEK and e.172 Batty. R.F.A. Waggon Lines. to Isolation Hosp. re measles cases at in Railway Operating Detachment — Weekly report	
"	14.1.17		To ST. JANS CAPELLE, inspected IX Corps Horse hip H.V.C. and 36 Divisional H.Q.	
"	15.1.17		To Water Lorry ST. JANS CAPELLE enquiry re personnel necessary to run same inspected 107. L.G. Co. transport lines & No. 2. Co. Div. Works Batt. Divisional Specialist School, & Sanitation Handover of same & 109 Rgde. H.Q. NEUVE EGLISE	
"	16.1.17		To 3 Canadian Tunnelling Co. re Blanket Sanitation, inspected Church Army hut NORTEPYP, A172 Batty. Waggon Lines. Thresh machine at NORTEPYP to disinfect 109 Rgde. blankets to 4th Guns. Lecture to IX Corps School of Sanitation IX Corps School of Sanitation, class taught instructional work in trench Sin latrines taken to inspect camp of 36 Bde. Hqrs & ROLFORD Camp.	
"	17.1.17			
"	18.1.17		To HYDEPARK CORNER and round 109 Rgde. trench sector also inspection of CATACOMBS, NORTEPYP camp, behind Army Hut. NORTEPYP.	

WAR DIARY
INTELLIGENCE SUMMARY

Army Form C. 2118.

Place	Date	Hour	Summary of Events and Information	Remarks and references to Appendices
BAILLEUL	19.1.17		To BAILLEUL infection hospital and with Capt Ellis Canadian. One to MONT NOIR about query diphtheria cases in civilians at DRANOUTRE & disinfection. Inspected 12 R.I.R. farms at METEREN.	
"	20.1.17		Inspected 10 R.I.R. & two transport lines, 109 Th.B. 14 R.I.R. transport lines, 9 R.I.R. & two transport lines, 11 R.I.R. transport lines & 109 M.G.C. - Weekly Sanitary report written up.	
"	21.1.17		L.C. 11 Lab. Ratt R.E. camp vacated yesterday left very dirty. Letter to Sanitary Sgnr. DRANOUTRE & ST JANS CAPELLE - sanitary "HQ".	
"	22.1.17		With Sanitary Sergt. inspected TYRONE FARM, MONMOUTH CAMP, WALLEFIELD HUTS transport lines of 1 S.R.I.R. & 10 R.I.R., YMCA HUT DRANOUTRE, 9 R.I.R. transport lines, ADS DRANOUTRE, & R.I.R. transport lines & NO. 2 Rest BAC	
"	23.1.17		To ALDERSHOT camp -11 R.I.R. re number case to other transport lines to 109 Rgte HQ. NEUVE EGLISE. Re disinfection - weekly - of CATACOMBS & ST JANS CAPELLE re attachment of Water lorry men to 76 San. Section. Lecture to 1st Corps School.	
"	24.1.17		With IX Corps School - constructional work, & later with them inspection of camp of 76 DSC TRULFORD Camp, Inspection 36 Div. HQ.	

Army Form C. 2118.

WAR DIARY
or
INTELLIGENCE SUMMARY.
(Erase heading not required.)

Instructions regarding War Diaries and Intelligence Summaries are contained in F.S. Regs., Part II. and the Staff Manual respectively. Title pages will be prepared in manuscript.

Place	Date	Hour	Summary of Events and Information	Remarks and references to Appendices
BAILLEUL S.17			Inspection of R. Irish Fus. transport lines, 12 R.I.R. transport lines, 108 of Co. transport lines, 36 Div. Specialist School, 36 Div. Advance Depot, 11 R.I.R. transport lines, 13 R.I.R transport lines.	
"	26.1.17		Having spent a.m. as per order had "Q" in office awaiting an inspection P.D. men on water duty, car did not come. Inspected 76 San. Sect. to METEREN to disinfect farms the occupied today by 9 R.I.R. inspection MONT NOIR IX Corps Officers rest station.	
"	27.1.17		to road to SP AMOUTHE inspecting, across country, to 36 Div. Specialist School the C.O. 12 Entrenching Batt. - Weekly Sanitary Report.	
"	28.1.17		to 108 F.A. no Inspection of Latrines men who have had to go with horse to CAPSTREE to same question. Sanitary Conference at HAZEBROUCK. Inspected NO.2 Co. AS.C. Siege train. Aldershot ALDERSHOT Camp - 15 P.I.R. (very bad) IX Horse disp. AFC, 36 Div. HQ + 36 Div. Signals.	
"	29.1.17		Camp at S.16.d. S.O. inspected to HYDERSHOT camps is necessary changes to 116 F.A. ADS. TROIS ROIS inspection instruction to O/C is taking & disinfecting of water wells issued in P.O. 1467, to 109 Pg. of HQ inspection arrangements	
"	30.1.17		disinfection HYDE PARK CORNER YPRES LODGE TROLFORD Camp the PEALE and through army hut NOP TEPYP on inspection.	

Army Form C. 2118.

WAR DIARY
or
INTELLIGENCE SUMMARY.
(Erase heading not required.)

Place	Date	Hour	Summary of Events and Information	Remarks and references to Appendices
BAILLEUL	5/1/17		With Lt Cpl School of Sanitation. Lecture demonstration. Kinematin to 150 Co R.E. inspection to M.O. & 1st P.I.R. re sterilization of water supply and inspection of Welsh Veterinary Section and 108 FA. Horse drawn to HAZEBROUCK to lecture on RATS at 2nd Army School of Sanitation	

"Confidential" Vol 517

40/99L
36 R.D

War Diary
of
Capt. E. Shrawson, R.A.M.C
O.C. 76th Sanitary Section.

February 1917.

COMMITTEE FOR THE
MEDICAL HISTORY OF THE WAR
Date 4 — APR. 1917

WAR DIARY
or
INTELLIGENCE SUMMARY.
(Erase heading not required.)

Army Form C. 2118.

Place	Date	Hour	Summary of Events and Information	Remarks and references to Appendices
BAILLEUL	1.2.17		Lecture and demonstrations to 2nd Army School of Sanitation Officers – 22 R.A.M.C at IX Corps School, and at BAILLEUL DUMP. and also at ALBERTA CAMP, RENINGHELST.	
"	2.2.17	afternoon	Inspected 71st Heavy Battery R.C.A Armm: col: WESTHOF FARM – "D" 153 R.F.A wagon Lines – No 1 Company D.A.C. – Inspected "C" 173 Battery R.F.A – Recommended changes in urinal and latrine arrangements. "B" 173 R.F.A – "K" Coy 15 R: I.R: RIFS: – Y.M.C.A hut, R.E. – ALDERSHOT CAMP. Latrine only for staff – very bad, BULFORD, no urinal. Party of 76th Sanitary Section detailed to do the necessary work, i.e build & screen urinal, build Incinerator & rectify latrine. "B" 172 Batty wagon Lines – Sanitation very good. 108 BDE H.Q. NEUVE EGLISE. Change necessary in latrine buckets – too low.	
"	3.2.17		BAILLEUL BATHS frozen out. Inspected drying, mending, ironing, disinfecting, also bathing rooms, PHINEGBOOM – 9 R.I.RIFS:	

Army Form C. 2118.

WAR DIARY
or
INTELLIGENCE SUMMARY.
(Erase heading not required.)

Place	Date	Hour	Summary of Events and Information	Remarks and references to Appendices
BAILLEUL	3.2.17		and adjacent farms – Sanitation as on previous visits – makeshift Latrines are not F.P and excreta are buried.	
"	4.2.17		1 case of German measles notified by M.O c/o 8th R.I.RIFS. Accompanied Capt Cheyne on tour of Inspection of MOULLE and surrounding villages occupied by 2nd Army School of Musketry.	
"	6.2.17		Lecture to IX Corps School of Sanitation on "Principles of Sanitation". Case of Scarlet fever notified by M.O 10th R.INNIS: FUS: Confirmed from B.I.H. Visited 109th Field Ambulance to make arrangements regarding segregation of S.F contacts. Visited HYDE PK CORNER and arranged with O.C 10 R.INNIS:FUS: (in absence of M.O) precautions being taken in dig-outs occupied in trenches and unit they are changing over with, and isolation of platoon when they come out. Made a Sanitary Inspection of same two. Inspected also CATACOMBS –	

WAR DIARY
or
INTELLIGENCE SUMMARY.

(Erase heading not required.)

Army Form C. 2118.

Place	Date	Hour	Summary of Events and Information	Remarks and references to Appendices
BAILLEUL	6.2.17		Inspected ENGLISH FARM – Sanitary condition unsatisfactory. Lecture to IX Corps school. Case of C.S.M notified in 10 R.I.R.	
"	7.2.17		With Sanitary School class to 36 A.S.C., A.S.C. sanitation good. Went on to BULFORD CAMP – Sanitation also good. Acinivised class. Inspected 108 M.G. COY. Also 107 M.G. COY Transport Lines. 108 T.M. BATTY. CHURCH ARMY HUT at KORTEYP. 172 BATTY, R.F.A. wagon lines also 12 R. IR. RIFS.	
		after-noon	Met A.S.C class at 79 Rue de Lille for Sanitary lecture re. Visited 76th Sanitary Section Camp with IX Corps Class. Cerebro Spinal Meningitis suspect notified from 10 R.I.RIFS. (not contact with other case on from that draft) – Notified 8.2.17 as P.U.O – not C.S.M – Negative R.U.O	
"	8.2.17		With R.A.M.C officers from 2nd Army School of Sanitation, lecture & demonstration at 79 RUE DE LILLE. Visited BAILLEUL DUMP	

Army Form C. 2118.

WAR DIARY
or
INTELLIGENCE SUMMARY.
(Erase heading not required.)

Instructions regarding War Diaries and Intelligence Summaries are contained in F. S. Regs., Part II. and the Staff Manual respectively. Title pages will be prepared in manuscript.

Place	Date	Hour	Summary of Events and Information	Remarks and references to Appendices
BAILLEUL	8.2.17	afternoon	and also ALBERTA CAMP, RENINGHELST. with them. Visited A.D.S. DRANOUTRE also NEW M.D.S. Inspected 9th R. INNIS: FUS: Transport Lines also 11 R. INNIS: FUS: Transport Lines. Sanitary arrangements improved since last visit. 109 M.G. COY — wrote O.C. regarding water supply — water should be boiled.	
"	9.2.17		Visited D.D.M.S IX corps to report progress sanitation Bailleul &c. Inspected "C" coy 1st Entrenching Batn Pioneer camp also RED LODGE — 9 R. Innis: Fus: Sanitary arrangements unsatisfactory. Inspected 36 D.A.C. H.Q. — Sanitation good. "B" Echelon D.A.C. Sanitary arrangements fairly good. 130 Batty R.G.A drew attention to several defects.	
"	10.2.17	afternoon	Visited 36 Div H. Qrs SAN JANS CAPELLE 11 R. INNIS: FUS: case of dysentry (suspect) Notified today	
			" " German Measles 107 T.M.B	
			" " Measles 108 M.G. COY	

Army Form C. 2118.

WAR DIARY
or
INTELLIGENCE SUMMARY.
(Erase heading not required.)

Instructions regarding War Diaries and Intelligence Summaries are contained in F. S. Regs., Part II. and the Staff Manual respectively. Title pages will be prepared in manuscript.

Place	Date	Hour	Summary of Events and Information	Remarks and references to Appendices
BAILLEUL	11.2.17		Notified by M. O. i/c 8th Entrenching Batt. of a case of Measles. Belgian child in Tea Room. Placed same "Out of bounds". Visited ESTAIRES – found various empty billets, Latrines and Incinerators in bad state; require to rebuild or vastly improved. Notified Town Major of same. Case of Scarlet fever notified in civilian, and one of Enteric in civilian – 4th in same house. Notified case of German measles suspect 11.R.I.RIFS: Rifleman 16.R.I.RIFS; taken off at HAZEBROUCK on way up to join unit as reinforcement, diagnosed as Scarlet fever.	
"	12.2.17		Accompanied D.D.M.S. IX Corps on tour of Inspection; visited ALDERSHOT CAMP Sanitation satisfactory. PALMER BATHS – Sanitary arrangements good. BULFORD CAMP – Suggested some improvements. DIVL CANTEEN and CHURCH ARMY HUT – Unsatisfactory. KORTEPYP CAMP – Pointed out improvements to be made.	

Army Form C. 2118.

WAR DIARY
or
INTELLIGENCE SUMMARY.
(Erase heading not required.)

Instructions regarding War Diaries and Intelligence Summaries are contained in F.S. Regs., Part II. and the Staff Manual respectively. Title pages will be prepared in manuscript.

Place	Date	Hour	Summary of Events and Information	Remarks and references to Appendices
BAILLEUL	12.2.17		Sent man 76 San. Sec. to disinfect dug-out from which German measles case was removed. Rifleman of 10 R.I.R. as C.S.M sent to B.I.H (suspect) second this week. This man was one of a draft of 144 men but not one of 21 contacts. Delivered lecture at IX Corps School.	
"	13.2.17		Inspected A.D.S. – DRANOUTRE also WAKEFIELD HUTS. RED LODGE visited – condition practically unchanged since last visit on which occasion wrote letter to "Q" branch drawing attention to insanitary state and Pioneer Camp latrines. CATACOMBS and HYDE PK COR the former fair, the latter sanitation good.	
"	14.2.17		Visited round H. Qrs. SAN VANS CAPELLE suggested some alterations. 36 Aird Signals R.E. Sanitation good. TYRONE CAMP – Sanitary arrangements good. 1 case German measles + one of Scarlet fever notified 14 R.I.R and 12 R.I.R respectively both	

T2134. Wt. W708-776. 500000. 4/15. Sir J.C. & S.

Army Form C. 2118.

WAR DIARY
or
INTELLIGENCE SUMMARY.
(Erase heading not required.)

Instructions regarding War Diaries and Intelligence Summaries are contained in F. S. Regs., Part II. and the Staff Manual respectively. Title pages will be prepared in manuscript.

Place	Date	Hour	Summary of Events and Information	Remarks and references to Appendices
BAILLEUL	14.2.19		10th sent to B.I.H. with IX Corps School of Sanitation. 36 D.S.C sanitation good. Inspected BULFORD CAMP, A.D.S TROIS ROIS. ALDERSHOT CAMP and arranged several matters re: Sanitation	
"	15.2.19		Saw Capt Cheyne re" several matters of importance and suggested improvements which were agreed to. Inspected VAUXHALL CAMP. ALDERSHOT CAMP. necessary alterations in last named to be carried out as soon as weather permits. 150 COY C.R.E sanitary arrangements far from satisfactory. Visited Camp Commandant SAN JANS CAPELLE about street urinal notices & pumping out of cess-pit.	
		After-noon	Inspected KORTEPYP CAMP. 107 T.M.B. 10 R:INNIS:FUS: 14 R.I.R Transport Lines. Arrangements made for improvements on the whole satisfactory. SHANKILL HUTS 12 R.I.R - Confirmed case of Scarlet fever. 30 contacts all H.Q men. Billets disinfected.	

WAR DIARY
or
INTELLIGENCE SUMMARY.
(Erase heading not required.)

Army Form C. 2118.

Place	Date	Hour	Summary of Events and Information	Remarks and references to Appendices
BAILLEUL	15.2.17		Wrote O.C detachment 10 R.I.R VAUXHALL CAMP re' water supply.	
"	16.2.17		Y.M.C.A hut DRANOUTRE visited. Sanitation good, but new urinal & new screen needed. 15 R.I.R. 10 R.I.R Transport Lines also 8th and 9th suggested some improvements. MONMOUTH CAMP. 122 COY and 7 Officers of 129 BATTY (Heavy) arrangements are in operation for latrines to change.	
	afternoon		In afternoon attended meeting of Medical Society at No 1 Canadian clearing Hosp. Wrote re' fouling of ground by German prisoners behind Camp 108th Field Ambulance.	
"	17.2.17		Saw O.C 108th Fd Amb. re Germ prisoners tot. Germ prisoners Camp NEERSECROM re fouling of ground by German prisoners. Made arrangements that dug-out latrines should be made where prisoners are working. Visited CHURCH ARMY HUT, KORTEPYP - No change yet in sanitary conditions. RED LODGE and H.P.C also visited.	

Army Form C. 2118.

WAR DIARY
or
INTELLIGENCE SUMMARY.
(Erase heading not required.)

Instructions regarding War Diaries and Intelligence Summaries are contained in F.S. Regs., Part II. and the Staff Manual respectively. Title pages will be prepared in manuscript.

Place	Date	Hour	Summary of Events and Information	Remarks and references to Appendices
BAILLEUL	18.2.17		Report to A.D.M.S. on arrangements for latrine accommodation of German prisoners working near 108th Field Ambulance. C.S.M. suspect 10 R.I.R. — diagnosed Influenza. Called at A.D.M.S. IX Corps Office to see M.A.D.M.S. re map reference for farm complained of by A.D.M.S. as wanting cheese. Visited MONMOUTH CAMP to see 122 COY R.E. as to who was in occupation of "cheese farm" at present, and in recent past. Went to "CHEESE" FARM T.3.C.95.73. found details from Infantry units of 36th Division there as working parties under R.E. — have been there 5 weeks but denied knowledge of use of that part of farm where cheese was found and still remained with other refuse..... Instructions given to bury cheese this afternoon. No R.E. there now: till 14 days ago some were in farm a little further down road in cellars..... 121 Coy R.E. were said to have been in occupation before them for 6 months. Report to A.M.D.S. written as above..—	

Army Form C. 2118.

WAR DIARY
or
INTELLIGENCE SUMMARY.
(Erase heading not required.)

Instructions regarding War Diaries and Intelligence Summaries are contained in F. S. Regs., Part II. and the Staff Manual respectively. Title pages will be prepared in manuscript.

Place	Date	Hour	Summary of Events and Information	Remarks and references to Appendices
BAILLEUL	19.2.17		Inspected RED LODGE – no improvement worth referring to noticed. HYDE PARK CORNER – no improvement here either. Accompanied by Capt. Picken R.A.M.C. visited subsidiary trenches RT SECTION on a tour of inspection. HUTTING COY CAMP – Camp Warden and one man were instructed to clean up two r.c., otherwise camp empty and clean. 171 Co R.E. – Corps Troops. Few latrines had lids. One or two not 3.P. (apart from lids). NO incinerator. No soak pit. Altogether this camp, which accommodates at present, 265 men, is in a very insanitary condition. Wrote letter to "Q" branch 2nd Army H.Q. on the subject. Visited also RAILWAY OPERATIONS DIV R.E. IX Corps. Room for improvement. Three cases of German measles notified. One from 9th R.I.R. in draft arriving from Zelitzbart 14 days ago. One case 15 R.I.R. and one R.G.A. man attached to E. Corps Siege Park.	

WAR DIARY
or
INTELLIGENCE SUMMARY.
(Erase heading not required.)

Army Form C. 2118.

Place	Date	Hour	Summary of Events and Information	Remarks and references to Appendices
BAILLEUL	20.2.17		Inspected "A" 153 Batty R.F.A Wagon Lines and found same in very insanitary state. Pointed out many defects. Visited RED LODGE and HYDE PARK CORNER. The sanitation of both leaves much to be desired. Lecture to IX Corps Sanitary School this afternoon. Notified today 2 Scarlet fever cases 1 – 9 R.I.R. 1 – 10 R. INNIS: FUS: also 2 Measles 1 – 13 R.I.R. 1 – 6 CAN: SIEGE "A" COL.	
"	21.2.17	after-noon	Inspected 3 Sections of 122 Coy R.E. NEUVE EGLISE also 108 Bde H. Qrs. X.Y.Z + V T.M.B – unsatisfactory. KANDAHAR FARM visited also WULVERGHEM. With IX Corps School of Sanitation to 36 D. S. A. Sanitation good. BULFORD CAMP – 9 R.I.R. satisfactory. In the evening delivered lecture on Sanitation to 36th Divisional School of Instruction at SAN MAIRE CAPELLE	
"	22.2.17		Accompanied A.D.M.S on tour of Inspection when the following camps were visited: HILLSIDE CAMP 16 R.I.R.	

Army Form C. 2118.

WAR DIARY
or
INTELLIGENCE SUMMARY.
(Erase heading not required.)

Instructions regarding War Diaries and Intelligence Summaries are contained in F. S. Regs., Part II. and the Staff Manual respectively. Title pages will be prepared in manuscript.

Place	Date	Hour	Summary of Events and Information	Remarks and references to Appendices
BAILLEUL	22.2.17		15 "O" Coy R.E. Much improvement in both these camps. MACHINE GUN BR: SPECIALISTS SCHOOL. DIV¹ SPECIALISTS SCHOOL. CAS BRANCH DIV¹ SPECIALISTS SCHOOL.	
		After-noon	German Prisoners camp, KEERSBROM. Sanitation in this camp excellent. Two men of Sanitary Section sent to Y.M.C.A tent BULFORD to complete work. Report most insanitary.	
"	23.2.17		Visited Y.M.C.A BULFORD CAMP Men of 76 Sanitary Section working party remedied all defects. Inspected X.Y.Z & V T.M.B - Ground much cleaner and work in progress. 108 Bde H. Qrs - Several improvements to be made. LYLO FARM - 12 R.I.R.-	
		After-noon	G.H.Q. 3ʳᵈ line of trenches N of firing point of range visited. No Latrine or Urinal yet erected. KORTEPYP visited, also RED LODGE and HYDE PARK CORNER. There is an improvement but much still remains to be done in two that named.	

Army Form C. 2118.

WAR DIARY
or
INTELLIGENCE SUMMARY.
(Erase heading not required.)

Instructions regarding War Diaries and Intelligence Summaries are contained in F.S. Regs., Part II. and the Staff Manual respectively. Title pages will be prepared in manuscript.

Place	Date	Hour	Summary of Events and Information	Remarks and references to Appendices
BALLEUL	24.2.17		Made an inspection of KORTEPYP CAMP – 13.R.I.RIFS: Improvements necessary. 160 S.F. contacts of 11.R.I.R are in this camp in a barn. Visited church Army Hut and Divisional Canteen. 107 T.M.B 10 R.INNIS: FUS: Transport Lines found much clothing at Incinerator including great coats, trousers, tunics shirts, fur coats, vests and drawers re-Equipment. Waterproof Sheets, Canvas buckets, Entrenching tools, Mess tins, Filled ammunition bandoliers &c. Wrote to "Q" re above. Measles hut 13 R.IR disinfected by 76 Sani: Sec: in this camp.	
"	25.2.17 SUN:		Inspected and planned out for Vegetable farming. 2 Huts – 25 × 55 – BULFORD CAMP disinfected where case of C.S.M. was. [struck through] Accompanied A.D.M.S. and Interpreter on tour. [struck through] 113 ARMY BDE R.F.A. now occupying Camps at or near DRANOUTRE vacated by 36 DIV UNITS	

T2134. Wt. W708–776. 500000. 4/15. Sir J.C.&S.

WAR DIARY
or
INTELLIGENCE SUMMARY.
(Erase heading not required.)

Army Form C. 2118.

Place	Date	Hour	Summary of Events and Information	Remarks and references to Appendices
BAILLEUL	25.2.17		and come under 36 DIVISION for Sanitary Administration	
"	26.2.17		SAN JANS CAPPEL – DIV: H.Q and CHATEAU inspected – satisfactory. 36 DIV: SIGNALS – Sanitation satisfactory. IX CORPS HORSE DIP A.V.C. Suggested various alterations. No 36 AMUNITION SUB PARK – Sanitation excellent. Men of 76 Sanitary Sec. disinfected farm X16 a. 08.47; at METEREN also disinfected meales of 15 R.I.R. All HUTS at VAUXHALL CAMP occupied by C.S.M contacts of 10 R.I.R. disinfected. This camp inspected; it has been left clean. ALDERSHOT CAMP – 9 R. INNIS: FUS: Suggested improvements are being carried out.	
		afternoon	36 DIV: AMUNITION SUB PARK WORKSHOP – alterations necessary. 1ST HALF CO No 1 INF: LABOUR CO D.N.I. – Sanitary arrangements bad. This unit only arrived late last night and consequently have had no time at disposal to put things in order.	

Army Form C. 2118.

WAR DIARY
or
INTELLIGENCE SUMMARY.
(Erase heading not required.)

Instructions regarding War Diaries and Intelligence Summaries are contained in F.S. Regs., Part II. and the Staff Manual respectively. Title pages will be prepared in manuscript.

Place	Date	Hour	Summary of Events and Information	Remarks and references to Appendices
BAILLEUL	27/3/17		Visited SAN JANS CAPPEL to inspect and report on methods of prevention of bad smell arising from midden, noticed in "Q" clerks office. The latrine was ventilated into the room — recommended ventilation to outside. Wrote "Q" branch to this effect. Inspected NEUVE EGLISE and 108 BDE H.Q. - work here well in hand. 171 Co. R.E. Improvements being carried out. Working party of 76th Sanitary Section employed making Urinal, Kitchen &c at 1st & Co. Inf. Lab. Co. D.L.I.	
		after noon	INKERMAN CAMP evacuated by 16 DIV - In very bad state. 12 R.IR.RIFS suspect case measles diagnosed S.F. Measles case reported 107 M.G.C. first being evacuated. Went on to KORTEPYP and phoned M.O. i/c unit occupying Camp to segregate all contacts and notify A.D.M.S office by wire when accomplished. Lecture to IX Corps School.	

Army Form C. 2118.

WAR DIARY
or
INTELLIGENCE SUMMARY.
(Erase heading not required.)

Instructions regarding War Diaries and Intelligence Summaries are contained in F. S. Regs., Part II. and the Staff Manual respectively. Title pages will be prepared in manuscript.

Place	Date	Hour	Summary of Events and Information	Remarks and references to Appendices
BAILLEUL	28/2/17		INKERMAN CAMP. KORTEPYP and camp occupied by 2ND & Coy No1 LABOUR Co D.L.I. Working party of 76th Sanitary Section employed cleaning up & repairing vacant camp INKERMAN. Building kitchen at ~~Kortepyp~~ and disinfect at No 1 LAB. CO. D.L.1 DRANOUTRE. Visited 105th BDE H.Q and NEUVE EGLISE. Sanitation progressing well 15 R.I.R Transport Lines. ~~Sanitation fairly~~ Unit only moved in recently. Sanitary improvements in operation. ENGLISH FARM. 107 BDE H.Q. Many improvements necessary. TROIS ROIS visited to ascertain work being done by Thresh machine. after noon IX Corps School to 36 D.S.C. - Sanitation good. BULFORD CAMP - Satisfactory. ~~cleaner than~~ previous to arrival of 76 Sam. Sec working party. INKERMAN CAMP. Much work still remains to be done. The following wells were disinfected today: 107 M.G.C.-1 ~~corps Signal of~~-2	

WAR DIARY
or
INTELLIGENCE SUMMARY.

Army Form C. 2118.

Place	Date	Hour	Summary of Events and Information	Remarks and references to Appendices
BAILLEUL	28/2/17		also see war 11 R.I.Rifs: KORTEPYP.	
			F. Sprawson Capt. R.A.M.C.	
			O.C. 76th Sanitary Section	

Confidential

War Diary

of

Capt E. C. Strawson R.A.M.C.T
O. C. 76th Sanitary Section

31st March 1917.

WAR DIARY
or
INTELLIGENCE SUMMARY.
(Erase heading not required.)

Army Form C. 2118.

Place	Date	Hour	Summary of Events and Information	Remarks and references to Appendices
BAILLEUL	1/3/17		10 R. INNIS: FUS: T.L. No ablution bench, otherwise clean. 11 R. INNIS: FUS: T.L. No ablution bench. New Incinerator in conjunction with drying room pulled down. Inis on ground opposite huts. 9 R. INNIS: FUS: T.L Food larder built by 8 R.I.R removed. Latrine to be moved to old concrete standings. Chloride of lime used in both urinal and latrine. 14 R.I.RIFS:T.L Latrine bucket standings to be cemented. No food larders in huts. Much cheese lying about in huts - wasted. New Incinerator in course of construction. A 153 BATTY R.F.A.W.L. — New camp - "Ayrshire" new urinal being made - Good camp (made by last occupiers) Drying room & Incinerator being constructed.	
		After-noon	36 DIVL SPECIALIST SCHOOL - Leaving here shortly for 2.5th Aierl School Mutvcen - vacated. O. Mess kitchen No 3. P larder not yet. GAS BRANCH of School - Urinal has been altered but still unsatisfactory. M.G BRANCH do - Latrine seats new F.P and A. 2 urinals raised but still unsatisfactory.	

WAR DIARY or INTELLIGENCE SUMMARY.

Army Form C. 2118.

Place	Date	Hour	Summary of Events and Information	Remarks and references to Appendices
BAILLEUL	1/3/17			
"	2/3/17		K Coy R.E. CELTIC PARK – New Incinerator finished – Camp good. Inspected 5 ENTRENCHING BATT^N. – Sanitation good. – 3 CANADIAN TUNNELLING CO: Good Camp. 13 R.I.R. T.L. – Alterations to be carried out in connection with Drying Room to — Notified of 2 cases German measles in 11 R.I.R. – KORTEPYP CAMP (leaving tonight) Hut disinfected by 76th Sanitary Sec; 11 R.I.R. T.L. – Incinerator still unaltered. 9 R.I.R. FUS. T.L. – Ablution bench to be improved. Notified to-day case of German measles in 11 R'IR'RIFS; also case of scarlet fever.	
"	3/3/17		RED LODGE – Much improved. CATACOMBS – to avoid any wet. HEGE PARK CORNER. Improved but sanitary arrangements of 2nd Army Field Survey Coy leave much to be desired. Hut occupied by S.F. case 9 R.I.R. disinfected by 76 San. Sec.	
"	4/3/17	SUN:	Visited civilian house where 2 children died of Diphtheria last week; swabs taken of 5 inmates. Infectious diseases notified to-day. – German measles 2. Measles 1. Suspect Diphtheria 1.	

WAR DIARY
or
INTELLIGENCE SUMMARY.
(Erase heading not required.)

Army Form C. 2118.

Place	Date	Hour	Summary of Events and Information	Remarks and references to Appendices
BAILLEUL	5/3/17		Inspected B 153 BATT R.F.A. W.L. D 173 BATT R.F.A. W.L.	
"	"		C 113 A.B. R.F.A. W.L. — Suggested improvements to be made	
"	"		in each. A 113 A.B. R.F.A. W.L. took H. No evap. grease-	
"	"		trap: tub used. to be altered. Alterations also necessary ablution	
"	"		bench, urinal and latrine, and not to use Chloride of lime	
"	"		B.A.C. 113 A.B. R.F.A. W.L. Food box required in Sgts mess. Cookhouse	
"	"		all food to be kept in Larder (cheese to was not) Latrines good, but	
"	"		use of Ch: of lime to be discontinued. Improvements suggested	
"	"		Urinal & Latrine @ Horse lines etc — B 113 A.B. R.F.A. W.L. ZOLLERN LINES.	
"	"		Billet of 2nd half No 1 LAB: Co: D.L.I. IX CORPS SIGNAL SCHOOL.	
"	"		Latrine being altered. Incinerator needs chimney. Billets V.G.	
"	"		VAUXHALL CAMP inspected & clean. H.Q 113 A.B. R.F.A. W.L. Satisfactory.	
"	"		Drinking water to be chlorinated. Letter to O/C to this effect.	
"	"		D 113 B A.B. R.F.A. W.L. Sanitation good. Notified today: German	
"	"		measles 1. Scarlet fever 2. Suspect C.S.M. 1.	
"	6/3/17		BULFORD CAMP visited. Improvements that should be made pointed out	

Army Form C. 2118.

WAR DIARY
or
INTELLIGENCE SUMMARY.
(Erase heading not required.)

Instructions regarding War Diaries and Intelligence Summaries are contained in F. S. Regs., Part II. and the Staff Manual respectively. Title pages will be prepared in manuscript.

Place	Date	Hour	Summary of Events and Information	Remarks and references to Appendices
BAILLEUL	6/3/17		108. M.G. Co: Latrines & urinal in bad condition - ALDERSHOT CAMP - 9 R. INNIS. FUS: visited in connection with C.S.M. prospect & necessary precautions taken.	
"	"	after-noon	DIV¦ SPECIALISTS SCHOOL - METEREN visited and letter written to "Q" regarding condition of same. Lecture to IX Corps School of Sanitation.	
"	7/3/17		In company of A.A.H.S visited Y.M.C.A BULFORD. CHURCH ARMY HUT. KORTEPYP. KORTEPYP - 13 R.IR. RIFS: Many changes necessary. 15 R.I.R T.L - 9 R.I.R T.L - 107 M.G. Co: Sanitation good. A.D.S - TROIS ROIS. Sanitation good. 171 Co' R.E. Not much work done here. NEUVE EGLISE - Much improved, but much still remains to be done, 108 BDE H.Q. New incinerators completed. Yards at backs of houses much tidier. Notified today of 2 cases mumps. German measles.	Temporary Sergeant
"	8/3/17		Visited Ant¦ Specialists School. METEREN. Work in progress. Temporary Incinerator and grease trap also erried by men of 76th Sanitary Sec: detachment 36 DIV= SIGNALS - WESTHOF FARM. Sanitation good. 1ST HALF No I LAB¦ Co' D.L.I Urinal built and other work at hands.	

T2134. Wt. W708—776. 500000. 4/15. Sir J. C. & S.

WAR DIARY
or
INTELLIGENCE SUMMARY.
(Erase heading not required.)

Army Form C. 2118.

Instructions regarding War Diaries and Intelligence Summaries are contained in F.S. Regs., Part II. and the Staff Manual respectively. Title pages will be prepared in manuscript.

Place	Date	Hour	Summary of Events and Information	Remarks and references to Appendices
BAILLEUL	8/3/17		TYRONE FARM 262 CO. R.E. Only a few days in possession. Some repairs to necessary. Wrote M.O. r/o chlorination of water.	
"	"		2ND ½ N° 1 CO: D.L.I. LAB: BATT: – No improvement in this camp other than that made by 76 Sanitary Sec: working party on 26.2.17.	
"	"		N° 2 SEC: D.A.C. Rubbish under huts (this hacking)	
"	9/3/17		Accompanied S.A.M.S. to N° 1 H.Q. C° A.S.C. Incinerator with drying room - good. Latrines tricked but not cemented to WESTHOF FARM. Sanitation good. HYDE PARK CORNER. – CATACOMBS and RED LODGE.	HYDE PARK CORNER
"	"		Fairly clean. Catacombs no change and RED LODGE unsatisfactory. Notified today of one case of Measles.	
"	10/3/17		Visited "Q" SAN JANS CAPPEL re bad smell and proposed remedy. PETIT PONT CABARET Many this still lying around. Instructions to bury. PIONEER CAMP vacated. Latrines left in filthy condition.	
"	"		X.Y.Z & V. T.M.B – Sanitation much improved & ground clean. F.P. & A Seat & lids supplied by 76 Sanitary Sec. to Y.M.C.A BULFORD and	
"	"		2 F.P. & A Seats & lids to R.O.D. ₪ unit NEUVE EGLISE 3 cases German measles notified today.	

Army Form C. 2118.

WAR DIARY
or
INTELLIGENCE SUMMARY.
(Erase heading not required.)

Instructions regarding War Diaries and Intelligence Summaries are contained in F. S. Regs., Part II. and the Staff Manual respectively. Title pages will be prepared in manuscript.

Place	Date	Hour	Summary of Events and Information	Remarks and references to Appendices
BAILLEUL	11/3/17	SUN:	Saw Capt Ellis, 5 Can: Mobile Lab: re C.S.M contacts.	
"	12/3/17		Accompanied A.M.S and Capt Crosbie re inspection 76th San:Sec	
"	"		Visited TYRONE FARM in connection with C.S.M contacts. Inspected	
"	"		A. 113 A. B.R. F.A. Waggon lines – Sanitation good. AYRSHIRE CAMP-"A"	
"	"		153 BDE R.F.A. New Incinerator now working – Sanitation good.	
"	"		Y.M.C.A DRANOUTRE Latrine for troops needed. 10 R.I.R. T.L	
"	"		Sanitary arrangements good. Camp found clean. 15 R.I.R. TL (took	
"	"		over from 14 R.I.R) camp clean. MONMOUTH CAMP 122 Co: R.E.	
"	"		262 Ry: Co: R.E. 2 SECTS & H.Q. 150 Co: R.E. Sanitation good. 76th San.	
"	"		Sec. disinfected 3 measles killed Mustapha Corner 15 R.I.R. (all officers and	
"	"		Hut 24 ALDERSHOT CAMP (C.S.M HUT) cases notified today: German	
"	"		measles 2: Mumps 1: Measles 2.	
"	13/3/17		Inspected BULFORD CAMP – 10 R: INNIS: FUS: Sanitation good. 108 BDE H.Q.	
"	"		NEUVE EGLISE. Sanitation & cleanliness of ground around much improved.	
"	"		Y.M.C.A BULFORD- Sanitation now good. 36 DIV: SPECIALISTS SCHOOL	
"	"		Several improvements noticeable. Notified today- Measles 2: German	
"	"		measles 2: Mumps 1.	

Army Form C. 2118.

WAR DIARY
or
INTELLIGENCE SUMMARY.
(Erase heading not required.)

Instructions regarding War Diaries and Intelligence Summaries are contained in F.S. Regs., Part II. and the Staff Manual respectively. Title pages will be prepared in manuscript.

Place	Date	Hour	Summary of Events and Information	Remarks and references to Appendices
BAILLEUL	14/3/17		With A.D.M.S. to PHINGBOOM & FARMS ADJACENT.— 11 R. INNIS. FUS: Took note of some alteration & improvement necessary. Lecture to IX Corps School of Sanitation in afternoon. The School attended at 76 San: Sec: Camp in readiness for instruction. IX Corps School of Signalling visited. Sanitation improving. 2 cases German measles notified. Manifesting party sent to 8 R.I.R.— H. FAR CORNER dugout from which infectious case being evacuated.	
	15/3/17		Inspected DONCASTER HUTS — 16 DIV: unsatisfactory state. 2ND HALF D.L.I LAB: CO. — under canvas. No sanitary arrangements of any kind. Working party under 76 SAN: SEC: to drain camp: drains to be cut. Many knapsacks. DERRY HUTS taken over from 16 Div: need improvements.	
		after- noon	Visited N° 36 AMUN: SUB: PARK A.S.C. — Sanitation good. IX Corps HORSE DIP A.V.C. Pointed out some changes. 36 DIV H.Q ST JANS CAPPEL Sanitary arrangements satisfactory. 36 D.S.C. A.S.C. Sanitation good. Notified today 9. Measles 1: C.S.M 1: Measles 1: Mumps 3:	

Army Form C. 2118.

WAR DIARY
or
INTELLIGENCE SUMMARY.
(Erase heading not required.)

Instructions regarding War Diaries and Intelligence Summaries are contained in F.S. Regs., Part II. and the Staff Manual respectively. Title pages will be prepared in manuscript.

Place	Date	Hour	Summary of Events and Information	Remarks and references to Appendices
BAILLEUL	16/3/17		Visited FLETRE - 109 BDE H.Q. Sanitary arrangements practically Nil. The same remarks apply also to COMTE CROIX - 13 R.I.RIFS.	
"	"		9 R:IR:FUS: CAESTRE "C" CO order to be provided for cookhouse, "A" CO. very clean — in house. "B" CO. and "D" CO. also inspected. Notified German measles 2. C.S.M. 2. DIV¹ SCHOOL (SPECIALISTS) billets disinfected.	
"	17/3/17		TYRONE FARM 107 M.G. CO: Barrn loft disinfected this morning. 2ND & N°1 LAB: CO: D.L.I. DRANOUTRE — Some drains have been cut, no further change. Water drawn from pump in DRANOUTRE & used unchlorinated: told to have it tested. Detach¹: N° 6 CO: D.L.I LAB:CO. 262 R⁴ CMP.R.E.	
"	"		CLAPHAM JUN. Much room for improvement. Improvements necessary.	
"	18/3/17	SUN:	Measles hut ALDERSHOT CAMP disinfected. Notified today of the following cases 9 R:INNIS:FUS: case measles. 10 R:IR:RIFS: 1 case measles	
"	19/3/17		Visited KEMMEL 8 R:IR:RIFS: BATT: H.Q. chateau in bad state. Cave heating used to chateau in a filthy condition.	

Army Form C. 2118.

WAR DIARY
or
INTELLIGENCE SUMMARY.
(Erase heading not required.)

Instructions regarding War Diaries and Intelligence Summaries are contained in F. S. Regs., Part II. and the Staff Manual respectively. Title pages will be prepared in manuscript.

Place	Date	Hour	Summary of Events and Information	Remarks and references to Appendices
BAILLEUL	19/3/17		Visited 262 Rly. Co. R.E. Slight improvement noticed. No 6 LAB Cº D.L.I. Suggested alterations. KEERSEBROM - R. SCOTS FUS: LAB Cº Camp in good condition	
"	20/3/17		In company with A.D.M.S. visited WAKEFIELD HUTS - 11 R.I.R. grease traps to be made either improvements carried out. DONCASTER HUTS. 12 R.I.R. Latrines, no seats, lids or backing. New grease traps to be made. No night urinals: no fire buckets. Wrote to "Q" re same.	
"	21/3/17		Lecture to IX Corps School of Sanitation. Notified memps 1. Inspected Nº 4 AMUN. SUB. PARK - Sanitation good. 13 R.I.R. T.L. genl. very good. Sanitary arrangements satisfactory. 13 R.I.R. "B" Cº Sanitation good. 36 D.A.C. - H.Q. D.A.C. Nº 2 SEC. Satisfactory. 87 BDE. R.F.A. H.Q "C" BATTY 87 BDE R.F.A. — 15 R.I.R. T.L. for both. His sanitary arrangements are good. Rt. HALF Nº 1 LAB Cº D.L.I. Many improvements necessary. LURGAN CAMP - 121 C.R.E. New latrine & cookhouse to be built. Alteration to Incinerant necessary. 16 R.I.R. good. 5 cases German measles evacuated today. 1 case recrudps notified.	

Army Form C. 2118.

WAR DIARY
or
INTELLIGENCE SUMMARY.
(Erase heading not required.)

Instructions regarding War Diaries and Intelligence Summaries are contained in F. S. Regs., Part II. and the Staff Manual respectively. Title pages will be prepared in manuscript.

Place	Date	Hour	Summary of Events and Information	Remarks and references to Appendices
BAILLEUL	22/3/17		Inspected 36 DIVL H.Q. also 9 R.I.R. FUSS. Visited 36 DIVL SPECIALISTS SCHOOL. Sanitation improving at Farms. At BREWERY. Latrines still bad. "D" BATTY 87 BDE R.F.A. Camp good. Improvements in progress. NEWMARKET CAMP. — 16 R.I.R. PIONEERS. DIVL HUTG CO. No incinerator. Cookhouse being built. Latrine TX Corps School of Sanitation. Notified today depth snopit - eventually stagnate tonsillitis. 2 cases. G. Measles 6. Mumps 1. Measles 1.	
	23/3/17		N. RIDING HEAVY BATTY (T) inspected. Improvements suggested. A 87 BDE. R.F.A. — AYSHIRE CAMP. unsatisfactory. DONEGAL FARM — 185 SIEGE BATTY R.G.A. Improvements necessary. Verminous — trousers clean clothing wanted & blankets disinfected. Notified to D.A.D.M.S. No. 1 SEC "B" C° 7 LABR BATT' R.E. Pond complained of by M.O. i/c in civilian — cannot be interfered with 48 MOBILE VET. SECTION. Sanitation good. Notified 2 cases G. MEASLES v 1 Measles.	
	24/3/17		335 RD CONSTL C° R.E. Moved in last night. Sanitary work to commence immediately under supervision of Sergt 76 SanL Sec 108 F.A. WAG. LINES and IX Corps Signal School. Sanitation good. also 36 DIVL REST STN.	

WAR DIARY
or
INTELLIGENCE SUMMARY.
(Erase heading not required.)

Army Form C. 2118.

Place	Date	Hour	Summary of Events and Information	Remarks and references to Appendices
BAILLEUL	24/3/19		107 BDE: H.Q. - 173 BDE: R.F.A. H.Q. Sanitation good, but ground on KEMMEL HILL much fouled. Notified German measles.	
"	"		Inoculated T.A.B. - ref.	
"	25/3/19 SUN		Notified today 1 case Mumps and one of Measles	
"	26/3/19		3 cases " 2 German measles	
"	27/3/19		Inspected 250 Co: R.E. TUNN: Co (16 DIV) KEMMEL and 9 R.I.R.H.Q.	
"	"		" KEMMEL CHATEAU. BEEHIVE DUG-OUTS (Latrines with canvas lid here good) REGENT ST dugouts. A.D.S LINDENHOEK - inspected " mukun road 27 A.S.S now clean. Lecture to IX Corps School of Sanitation	
"	28/3/19		visited in company with A.A.M.S KEERSEBROM CAMP to select & plan site of new camp of 2 R. SCOTS LAB: BATT.N. Detachment 107 M.G. CO. Much refuse by hedge. Instructed to have cleared up. 335 R.D. CONST.N CO. R.E. No material yet available - letter to "Q" Detachment - B. CO. 7 LAB: BATT.N R.E. Good. Nos 1, 2 & 3 COs A.S.C. DIV: TRAIN. H.Q. A.S.C. & 48 MOBILE VET. SECT.N. Newly arrived camp in making - taken over	

Army Form C. 2118.

WAR DIARY
or
INTELLIGENCE SUMMARY.
(Erase heading not required.)

Place	Date	Hour	Summary of Events and Information	Remarks and references to Appendices
BAILLEUL	28/3/17		from 13 R.I.R. & y three from 16 DIVN last week. Notified Measles 3. German measles 2.	
"	29/3/17		Visited KEERSEBROM & NEW CAMP to be occupied by 2. R. SCOTS LABR. CO. Incinerators to be built on new camp site today.	
"	"		TYRONE FARM – 107 M.G. CO. Changes necessary. 107 T.M.B. Billet good & clean also Cookhouse. New latrines being made. 1ST HALF	
"	"		No. 1 LAB: CO: – D.L.I. A very bad camp. Lecture to IX Corps School of Sanitation. Notified today. M(easles 1. German measles 1.	
"	30/3/17		262 RLY: CO: R.E. Much need for improvements. 2ND HALF No 6 CO. D.L.I. Sanitation bad. CELTIC PARK K. CO: R.E. Sanitation good Y.M.C.A. Sanitation satisfactory. KEERSEBROM CAMP In process of evacuation. 2ND R. SCOTS LABR CO New camp in process of completion & very good. IX Corps HORSE DIP. A.V.C. Sanitation satisfactory. 36 D.S.C. A.S.C. Sanitation very good. 36 DIV H.Q. Sanitation do 36 DIV SIGNALS " good. Notified today German measles 5. Mumps 1.	

Army Form C. 2118.

WAR DIARY
or
INTELLIGENCE SUMMARY.
(Erase heading not required.)

Place	Date	Hour	Summary of Events and Information	Remarks and references to Appendices
BAILLEUL	31/3/17		36 DIV: GAS SCHOOL: N.31 C10.1 Latrines open pits in billet. Cookhouse No F.B. Latrines No lids – this only. 76 San: Sec. to clean up. CAMP OF R SCOTS FUS: and CAMP OF WORKING PARTIES 12 & 13 R.I.R. & 9 R.I. FUS; visited. Improvements necessary. 76 San: Sec: to clean up the latter. KEERSEBROM CAMP. Sanitation good. 76 San: Sec: party cleaning DRANOUTRE ROAD. Disinfection – 2 men sent to 107 BDE H.Q to disinfect for German measles. Notified today German measles 3 cases.	

F. C. Sprawson. Capt.
O.C. 76 Sanitary Section.
31.3.17.